THE LITT

Kitti Cha Sangmanee
Catherine Donzel
Stéphane Melchior-Durand
Alain Stella

Flammarion

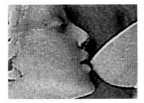

Heat up some water, toss a teabag in your cup and start drinking—or screw off the top of the latest iced tea beverage and take a chug. Tea connoisseurs will shake their heads and cry blasphemy, for this goes against all the rules of tea-drinking. How should tea be prepared? What is the secret of great tea?

Over the past few centuries the consumption of tea has spread throughout the entire world. Its production is more and more industrialized. How does the art of drinking tea fit into this picture? Has the taste of tea evolved over time?

Tastes in tea vary from China to England, India to the Mediterranean, and Russia to Kenya. Yet so rich in traditions, and convivial by nature, might not the art of drinking tea be a bridge linking different cultures?

A N S W E R S

Orientation p. 6

The alphabetical entries have been classified according to the following categories. The categories are indicated with a small colored rectangle.

■ Types of Tea:
great traditional
varieties,
classifications,
blends and
new creations.

■ Tea and Life:
fabrication,
atmosphere
and environment,
kinds of taste.

■ History:
historical facts
and events,
economic contexts,
human involvement
and adventures.

The information given in each article, together with cross-references indicated by asterisks, within parentheses, and with colored squares will help you to explore the world of tea.

The Story of Tea p. 11

A detailed overview of the themes and information provided in the alphabetical entries.

Alphabetical Guide p. 27

In alphabetical order, the entries tell you everything you need to know to journey through this fascinating world. The information is enriched with detailed discussions of all the major varieties of tea, historical information, and essential savoir-faire for connoisseurs.

I. DISCOVERY AND EXPANSION

A. The Tea Route

Starting in China and voyaging first in trading caravans and then along maritime routes, tea gradually conquered Western tastes. Once its closely guarded production and fabrication methods were uncovered, the colonial powers made every effort to cultivate and produce tea wherever climatic conditions permitted. In the nineteenth century, exhibitions at world's fairs did much to increase the popularity of tea-drinking among the general public.

Boston Tea Party	*Loolecondera*	*Transplantation*
Caravan	*Maritime Trading Companies*	*World's Fairs*
Clipper	*Trading Post*	

B. Western Commerce Begins

Tea production remained a secret for thousands of years until a bold English botanist managed to steal it from China in the nineteenth century. The perseverance of Western pioneers led to the spread of tea cultivation, its consumption throughout the world, and the rise of several families to fame and fortune.

Bruce Brothers	*Lipton, Thomas*	*Taylor, James*
Exoticism	*Pioneer*	*Twining, Thomas*
Fortune, Robert		

C. The Tea Business

Although the production and manufacture of superior teas still requires intricate work by experienced cultivators, more and more large tea companies use industrial processes. Each year, harvest quality is evaluated by skilled tea-tasters and the consumer is continually presented new products on the international market.

■ *Conditioning*	■ *Industry*	■ *Tasting Expert*
■ *Consumption*	■ *Statistics*	■ *Textured and Crafted Teas*
English Passion		

II. HOW THE GARDEN GROWS

A. Great Tea Gardens

Soil quality and climatic conditions are determining factors in the taste of the many different kinds of tea. Therefore, knowing where a tea comes from is indispensable for choosing the right one and recognizing superior blends.

- *Assam*
- *Ceylon*
- *China*
- *Darjeeling*
- *Formosa*
- *India*
- *Indonesia*
- *Japan*
- *Kenya*
- *Korea*
- *Vietnam*

B. Making Tea

Tea cultivation takes place on plantations called "gardens," and the quality of the tea depends on how the leaves are harvested. Manufacture almost always takes place in very close proximity to plantations, and requires five specific and painstaking procedures.

- *Camellia sinensis*
- *Climate*
- *Conservation*
- *Desiccation*
- *Fermentation*
- *Garden*
- *Gathering*
- *Manufacture*
- *Production*
- *Rolling*
- *Sifting*
- *Withering*

C. Classifying Tea

Teas are classified by color and by harvesting methods. Black tea leaf grades are indicated on containers and tea bags by a series of initials. Choosing a good tea requires an understanding of this classification system.

- *Black*
- *Classification*
- *Green*
- *Gunpowder*
- *Semi-fermented* .
- *Smoked*
- *White*

III. TEA DRINKING

A. Ingredients for a Nice Cup of Tea

Teas can be enjoyed in many forms, following different rituals, and with the use of various utensils. There are also a great variety of blends, flavors, scents, and so on.

- *Lemon*
- *Milk*
- *Porcelain*
- *Preparation*
- *Sugar*
- *Tea Sets*
- *Teapots*
- *Water*
- *What to Drink When*

B. The Taste of Tea

There are as many flavors as there are teas, whether they are made to ancient recipes or are the products of the latest technological advances. Teas are named with a precise and poetic vocabulary. Very often they are drunk unblended and unflavored, though certain blends are delicious.

- *Aromatized*
- *Blends*
- *Flavored*
- *Iced*
- *Mint*
- *Russian*
- *Smoked*
- *Textured and Crafted Teas*

C. Tea Times

Tea time is not at five o'clock sharp everywhere. But whenever it takes place, individually or with others, it is always a relaxing moment. In the West, tea was long consumed by, and associated with, the upper classes. In the Far and Middle East, however, tea drinking has deep roots in all classes.

- *Europe*
- *France*
- *Orient*
- *Samovar*
- *Tea Room*
- *Tea Time*
- *Tibet*
- *United States*

IV. THE ESSENCE OF TEA

A. An Art of Living

From its beginnings in China tea has been closely associated with high culture, and therefore the fabrication and consumption of tea has always been an indication of a cultivated lifestyle. Tea has played an important part in popular, classical, and scientific literature. In Japan, tea preparation has been associated with a codified tea ceremony for centuries. For some people, drinking tea is a ritual and even a reflection of their personal philosophy.

▨ *European Literature*   ■ *Ritual*   ■ *Tea Ceremony*
■ *Fortune-Telling*   ■ *Schools*   ■ *Zen*
▨ *Legend*

B. The Virtues of Tea

Medicinal qualities have been ascribed to tea for thousands of years. Like all plants, tea possesses particular properties: modern science is beginning to explore and make use of the traditional beliefs in the benefits of drinking tea.

■ *Composition*   ■ *Theine*
■ *Health*   ▨ *Treatises*

THE STORY OF TEA

"Drink a cup of tea and forget the cares of the world." So stated T'ien Yiheng, well before connoisseurs around the globe came to know the object of his passion—a passion that makes the thirst for gold seem trifling.

"Sublime libation, your origin is celestial!" Legend* has it that the very first drops of tea in the world moistened the lips of the divine Emperor Chen Nung. The earliest beverage known to humankind, tea's noble history extends back five thousand years and is punctuated with fascinating personalities, fierce battles, and major political upheaval. Tea is the most widely consumed beverage on the face of the earth. Its virtues are well known: tea heals, quenches, and sustains.

But its secret powers reside in its almost human qualities. Tea tells stories, punctuates journeys, and is a muse to poets. Tea brings cultures together and is a sign of hospitality and conviviality. Over the centuries no other earthly product has called forth such subtle and intricate rituals. The materials required for serving tea are often of supreme elegance. Tea brings people together in times of trauma. The history of tea is inextricably intertwined with the history of humanity.

I. Discovery and Expansion
A. The Tea Route

From its discovery until the beginning of the seventeenth century tea was unknown in the West. China was the dominant producer, and only very slowly did agricultural production make its way to Korea,* Tibet,* and Japan.* Oases and caravans on the silk route provided a first bartering point, but distribution and trade remained highly restricted.

While its traditions were anchored to the earth, the tremendous commercial expansion experienced by tea in the seventeenth and eighteenth centuries took place on the high seas. English, French, and Dutch maritime* trade companies went to great lengths to secure agreements and to establish commercial relations with the resistant, intr$actable Chinese. The history of these efforts is rife with underhand maneuvers, ruthless traders, and strokes of genius. George III of England's strategy was to "cultivate friendship with China" by introducing opium into the theater of operations, thus tipping the balance of credits and payments in favor of his own glory and the East India Company's coffers. Thus tea brought England success in the East; but in the West it led to revolution. The symbol of cordiality and hospitality became that of liberty and independence for Americans with the Boston* Tea Party—an inaugural act of the Revolutionary War.

Eventually clippers and steamships accelerated distribution, yet they could not keep up with consumer demand for this "exotic"* product. The next strategic move was to take control of production. Thus the British Empire created plantations in India and then Ceylon (present day Sri Lanka).

European Merchant Purchasing Tea in China. Eighteenth century. Watercolor. Victoria and Albert Museum, London.

B. Western Commerce Begins

Of course, this conquest did not take place without difficulty. Romantic versions depict voyages along the Brahmaputra River and plantation owners on elephant-back. But colonization was a tough business; an unrelenting struggle with the jungle, wild animals, illness, isolation, and back-breaking hard work.

In 1849, Robert Fortune* traveled through China on a sedan chair. He disguised himself first as a Chinese merchant and then as a Mongol mandarin. His mission: to uncover the secret of tea production for the king. Thanks to Fortune, twenty thousand "tea tree" saplings were planted in the Himalayan foothills. Ceylon later adopted cultivation of Assam plants from India, becoming the "island of tea."

Such pioneers* gave way to gentlemanly tea merchants. Founded in the eighteenth century, Twining* became a principal tea broker in the following century. In the early twentieth century, the charismatic Thomas Lipton* appeared on the scene with his daring and genius for public relations. He dispensed with middlemen in sales of his Ceylon tea, making it affordable for the masses.

C. The Tea Business

Today, nearly forty countries grow tea, from Argentina to Zimbabwe. The main producers are also the primary consumers. Tea is a business worth three billion dollars a year. Industrialization has replaced golden clippers with legg-cutters, and tea leaves are cut, crushed, and inserted into paper tea bags in a flash—all by machine.

Two and a half million tons of tea are produced each year. Tea brokers operate out of the Colombo, London, and Calcutta commodity exchanges. More than two billion cups of tea are drunk around the world every day.

But old traditions have not entirely vanished. Hand-produced quality tea is still in high demand and remains the standard of market excellence. The traditional tea purveyors provide expertise and ensure the continued availability of the finest teas. Tea-based health, beauty, and culinary products are a new and expanding market.

II. How the Garden Grows
A. Great Tea Gardens

In loose, deep, acid soil, at high altitude, where summer and autumn rains feed well drained ground, in the heat, with little wind, where morning fog wraps the mountains, and other plants die, *Camellia* * *sinensis* flourishes in a setting of natural splendor.

Tea chests, China, nineteenth century. Musée du Thé, Mariage Frères, Paris.

There are thousands of tea gardens.* Some plantations extend over entire regions. In Assam* alone, there are two thousand gardens, some of them extending over two thousand acres. There are more gardens in China* than there are vineyards in France.

Though industrial production has resulted in a standard quality in China, exceptional teas are still cultivated, and their richness is beyond compare. Yin Zhen (Silver Needles), the most precious white tea, is harvested only two days of the year. Pei Hou, a smooth green tea, grown in a garden that can be reached only by trekking on foot for five hours, is gathered but once a year. Such exceptional teas as Fenghuang Dancong, a semi-fermented Gungdong master-piece, or the black orchid-scented Keemun Moafeng (From the Lion's Mountain) make China, with its secret gardens, a veritable treasure trove. Formosa, with its wonderful Oriental Beauty Oolong tea, is not far behind.

The greatest black teas are grown in the Darjeeling* region, which boasts eighty-seven first-rate gardens. The soil gives this tea a subtle Muscat flavor. The finest estates include Castleton, Namring, Margaret's Hope, Ambootia, Puttabong, and the mysterious garden of Arya, whose autumn harvest bears the incomparable scent of Himalayan Rose. Darjeeling teas are classified according to when they are gathered: first flush, in-between, second flush, or autumnal. According to season, teas are more or less flowery, fruity, or ripe in flavor.

Japan* has its own tea masterpieces. Gyokuro (Precious Dew), the world's foremost green tea, is shaded by mats for three weeks before harvesting.

This delectable journey through the enchanting and complex world of tea covers the whole globe, from the vast gardens of Assam, under the dazzling Sri Lankan* sun, to the volcanic slopes of Mount Cameroon and beyond.

B. The Making of Tea

A mature tea plant can reach up to sixty feet in height, making bud gathering a difficult prospect. When grown in nurseries, the plants may be pruned to a size shorter than the tea gatherers, who are usually women.

Gatherers of Ceylon tea perform the gestures of leaf picking fifty thousand times a day, plucking the uppermost leaves with expert gentleness. Their livelihood depends on it. They toss the leaves over their shoulders into wicker baskets on their backs. Each step of tea production is carefully regulated at a nearby processing plant.

Certain aspects of fermentation* remain a mystery. This chemical reaction depends on the skill of the technician, who must determine the precise moment to stop for optimal results. The delicate interaction between human sensitivity and the forces of nature explains why no two batches of tea, even from the same garden* and harvest, are identical. This makes that taste of tea all the more beguiling.

C. Classifying Tea

Camellia sinensis is the sole species of tea grown today. It consists of a number of hybrids. Differences in processing, quality, preparation, and harvest time are the bases for the creation of categories to classify tea's infinite subtleties.

The Chinese were the first to set up distinctions based on infusion color: white, green, or red, which were then considered in terms of intensity. They also classified white and green teas—which are unfermented—from semi-fermented,* scented, compressed, and black* or fermented tea.

Black tea is the most popular in the West, and is subject to a Western classification* system which takes processing methods and degrees of fermentation into account. Black tea is categorized according to the type of gathering* and the flavor's strength. The terms F.O.P., G.F.O.P., S.F.T.G.F.O.P., and so forth express a wealth of information to connoisseurs. Those who prefer stronger tea will tend to choose broken leaves, symbolized by B. in the appellation.

The system accounts only for black tea. Other teas are classified according to the appearance of their leaves: flat (Lung Ching), rolled in a ball (Gunpowder), twisted (Formosa Oolong), or crafted into textured forms (resembling flowers, stars, pearls, etc.) The younger the buds and leaves, the higher the quality.

III. Tea Drinking
A. Ingredients for a Nice Cup of Tea

Tea is exacting. Each infusion has its own character, nature, and secrets. Poor preparation* can ruin leaves from even the best garden. Success is a question of attention to codes, and of a certain degree of experience.

Textured teas, from top to bottom: *Huang Shan Bouquets, Hu Bei Tea Buds, Hu Bei Tea Stars, Tuo Cha Lubao, Tea Pearls.*

The right water releases tea's full flavor and aroma. If it is too hard, chlorinated, high in fluoride, or if it contains sediments, the water will ruin the tea. Only very pure water will do. In his famous eighth-century work *Chaking* (*Tea Classic*), Lu Yu sets up a hierarchy of types of water, with mountain water at the top, followed by river and then spring water.

The choice of teapot also merits careful consideration. Porcelain* or enameled cast iron pots are suitable for most teas. Glass pots, which do not hold the tea's flavor, are fine for scented tea, and metal (pewter or silver) teapots complement strong, tannin-rich teas. Some consider clay teapots from Yixing, in the Chinese province of Jiangsu, to be ideal. Yixing pots become "seasoned" rapidly and retain the full flavor of the tea. But such seasoned teapots should not be used for different types of tea. Connoisseurs employ different pots for every type of tea: black, smoked black, semi-fermented, and scented. A teapot with an internal filter is useful; otherwise a cotton strainer will do.

Water temperature is crucial. Long boiling ruins the water, destroys the leaves, and spoils flavor. Water should be just before the boiling point, and cooled slightly for delicate green and white teas. Use two and a half to three and a half grams (approximately one teaspoon) of black or semi-fermented tea per cup; four and a half to ten grams for green or white tea.

Finally, the key to making a good cup of tea is in its brewing. The time required for this depends on whether the leaves are crushed, broken or whole and also varies according to the type of tea: green, semi-fermented, First Flush Darjeeling etc. Brewing must be ended—that is, the leaves should be taken out—just as the aromas and tannins are released.

B. The Taste of Tea

The vocabulary of tea is pure poetry. Like wine, tea is described by its color: green, amber, golden, brown; its flavor: flowery, round, aromatic, sweet; its liquor: limpid, crystalline, brilliant.

The variety of tea flavors, catering for the sweet-toothed and the savory-toothed alike, suggests to what extent taste is a question of background. Japan's tradition is based only on green tea. Chinese teas are primarily green or semi-fermented. The rarity of sugar* in remote regions of Central Asia leads some tribes to temper its flavor with salt and yak butter.

Green and Oolong teas were the first to reach Europe. But Western tastes strongly favor black tea, whose round flavor goes well with both salty and sweet foods. The English adopted strong black tea from Assam and Ceylon—teas that could be enjoyed with a drop of milk. This preference spread throughout Europe.

Reproduction of a silver oriental-style teapot from 1875. Musée du Thé, Mariage Frères, Paris.

France has forged its very own tea drinking culture since then. Today, the array of choice offered to French tea aficionados is among the greatest in the world: rare white teas; prestigious green teas; over fifty Darjeeling teas; pickings from all seasons and the very finest selections. Each moment of the day—morning, afternoon and evening—calls for a different tea. Like wine, tea should complement the taste of the food it accompanies: for white meats, a Lapsang Souchong; for spicy dishes, a lotus green tea…

Gourmet inclinations contribute to an art of blending and the creation of teas—classic or scented—with original twists, reflecting individual tastes. This inventive flair is the true hallmark of French tea-making.

Tea leaves.

The education of the palate is a gradual process and might well begin with scented or blended teas, progressing to black tea of varying strengths, then black teas from great gardens and different harvests, followed by semi-fermented tea, first from Formosa and then China, China green, the Japan green teas, and finally white tea.

C. Tea Times

"When will the West understand—or try to understand—the East? Strangely enough, humanity has so far met in the tea-cup. It is the only Asiatic ceremonial which commands universal esteem." So said Okakura Kakuzo.

Following page: Singhalese man transporting tea.

Regardless of cultural differences, tea brings people together. In the East, it is omnipresent: at village hostels in China, in tiny Egyptian cafés, in stations and trains, in Bedouin tents, and from street vendors. All kinds of business are conducted and the most secret of secrets may be shared over a cup of tea. Tea reaches across the generations.

Tea can also constitute a meal, as with the English traditional high tea. The English drink tea at all times of the day, and in moments of crisis, when it truly transcends social categories.

In Western culture, tea still bears the mark of its aristocratic origins. In France, tea is still regarded as a foreign treat, but is gaining ground rapidly: while all over the world outstanding artisans create elegant tea sets and chefs produce tea-based gourmet delights.

IV. The Essence of Tea
A. An Art of Living

Tea bridges the gap between very different cultures and lifestyles encountered across the world.

Ever since the eighth-century publication of Lu Yu's *Chaking* or *Tea Classic*, tea has been a part of intellectual and artistic life in China. Written during the T'ang Dynasty (618–907), this book was both a revelation and a revolution. From being a simple beverage, tea became a spiritual elixir, the subject of poems and paintings, a topic of reflection, and the pretext for courteous disputes up and down the Blue River. Under the Song Dynasty (906–1279) the art of tea reached the very highest refinement, aiming for utter perfection.

Japan, in its turn, developed a whole philosophical universe around tea. Architecture, landscaping, calligraphy, and flower arrangement are all indispensable elements of the tea ceremony.* Tea utensils are lovingly crafted to be symbols of Zen culture and capture that which is beautiful. Tea is a threshold from the everyday world to the divine.In Morocco and neighboring countries, mint* tea is a sign of hospitality. Travelers are welcomed with this nectar that the Touareg tribesmen say is "bitter as death, sweet as life, and tender as love."

For the English, tea gardens are the site where tea meets the Gainsborough landscape in perfect bucolic delight: elegant London hotels provide delicious afternoon teas where one can partake of a fine Darjeeling or Lapsang Souchong before dancing the evening away to the sound of a string quartet.

In the United States, tea is first and foremost a symbol of the country's blow for liberty with the Boston Tea Party. Nowadays, however, the grudge has been forgotten, and numerous English-style tea rooms are found across the continent, from the refined Lady Mendl's Tea Salon in New York to the coziest small-town restaurant serving home-made cakes to enjoy with the tea.

B. The Virtues of Tea

Under the Han Dynasty (206 B.C.–A.D. 220), the Chinese had already discovered tea's pharmacological properties; they drank it to counteract fatigue, uplift spirits, fortify willpower, and improve eyesight. Europeans have also been studying its effects for some time. For instance, Philippe-Sylvestre Dufour described how "the excellent beverage cures headaches" in his *Tea Treatise** of 1685.

Since then, researchers have discovered the presence of theine* and theophylline, accounting for tea's specific stimulant and diuretic effects; flavonoids, which reduce cholesterol and lower blood pressure; as well as pre-tannins, fluoride, antiseptics, and Vitamin C. Medical and cosmetic research regularly uncover new merits of green tea.

Tea's beneficial qualities are universally acknowledged.

Welcome to the world of tea.

Kitti Cha SANGMANEE

Traditional
Japanese
iron teapots.
Mariage
Frères, Paris.

▪ Aromatized

Aromatized teas are part of a time-honored tradition, but the vogue for a whole range of flavored teas is a recent development, spreading through Europe from France and Germany in the 1970s. It is impossible to classify the range of flavors available, including every imaginable fruit, spice, and condiment, as well as a range of  flowers and liqueurs. The purist, who savors the subtle essence of a particular "garden"* or the complex balance of a perfect blend with each sip, might dismiss these creations as mere tea-based infusions. However, these products, which represent a third of all sales for the finest producers, continue to attract a new clientele (for the most part women and young people) to the world of tea, via strong, fruity flavorings. Aromatization is performed in a rotating drum, which sprinkles the leaves with essences or essential oils. Flower petals, fruit zest, or slivers of peel are often added for primarily aesthetic reasons. In Europe, teas flavored with natural essences are preferred, and legislation prohibits the use of synthetic aromatization. AS

Left:
Annamite man in Hanoi smoking a pipe while his tea steeps, c. 1915. Albert Kahn Collection, Boulogne-Billancourt, France.

Below:
A tea gatherer at work in Assam, northeastern India.

▪ ASSAM: LAND OF TWO THOUSAND GARDENS

Tucked in between the Himalayas and Mounts Naga and Patkoi, the Assam region covers the valley of the Brahmaputra River in northeast India. This region was a dense jungle in the nineteenth century, before wild tea plants were discovered and the area was cleared by English colonists. Today, Assam remains one of the least populated Indian states. During the monsoon season, from April to September, the temperature rises to 95°F (35°C), creating an immense natural greenhouse, in which nearly a third of all Indian tea is grown. This major tea-producing area numbers over two thousand gardens. The most illustrious include Bhooteachang, Dikom Gold, Hattiali, Napuk,  Numalighur, and Rungagora. These gardens can be as large as two thousand acres, extending under large shade-providing trees. The rain-resistant Assam tea plants produce large leaves. The climate, insects, and snakes make plantation work hard in this region, especially during the harvest season, from May to January. Assam teas are strong, astringent, and fresh to the palate, and they hold up well to a splash of cold milk. These are the basic characteristics of all traditional British blends. AS

■ BLACK: THE TEA THAT WON THE WEST

Black or fermented tea appears to be a Western taste. It represents the entire production of the former British colonies of India* and Ceylon,* and in China it is reserved exclusively for export. The story that black tea comes from the accidental fermentation of Chinese green* tea during a long journey is likely based in legend. All black teas are characterized by a colored infusion, from pale orange for a First Flush Darjeeling, to reddish brown for Kenya tea. Black teas are full-bodied yet mild. Generalities aside, the teas vary greatly from one country to the other.

China boasts a great variety of black teas, a handful of which are smoked.* The round, full-bodied, "grand" Yunnan teas are nick-named the "mocha of tea" for their rare combination of aroma and strength. The lighter Keemun teas are known for their orchid taste. These teas are sold whole-leaf.

The black teas of India and Ceylon are available in different leaf grades (see Classification) ranging from mild to strong in taste. This British notion is highly relative. Darjeeling teas, for example, vary in accordance with the time of gathering.* Spring Darjeelings are as fresh and light as semi-fermented teas. Ceylon teas are potent in the case of Broken Orange Pekoe (B.O.P.) and Fannings, and make delicate aromatic infusions in whole-leaf varieties, including Flowery Orange Pekoe (F.O.P.) and Orange Pekoe (O.P.) Assam* teas are malty and strong, with a dark liquor. The majority of commercially available classic blends* use black teas. The best-known British-inspired blends are a mix of the three great production regions, China, India, and Ceylon. Assam* and Ceylon teas are often blended in B.O.P. for breakfast teas, or in whole-leaf form for lighter afternoon teas. In recent years, tasters have developed such refined and unexpected blends as Darjeeling and Assam for brunch teas, as well as delicate Darjeeling and Yunnan mixes. CD

Black teas, from top to bottom: *Taloon*, T.G.F.O.P., Indonesia. *Misiones*, B.O.P., Argentina. *Jamirah*, G.F.B.O.P., Assam, India.

■ Blends

The art of blending is the tea-taster's science. These professionals combine different quality teas for product standardization, to ensure stable flavors and prices. They are the secret behind the consistency of flavors. Like the expert "noses" in the perfume industry, tasting* experts sometimes invent new aromas, blending great garden* varieties in perfect proportion to obtain original results. "Classic" blends, which skillfully combine the aromas of diverse teas, are the most difficult to achieve. They are significantly more delicate than the flavored blends that add flower or fruit aromas to tea.

In addition to talent and intuition, blenders follow certain guidelines. Teas with strong personalities should never be blended, because each destroys the other's character. It is best to start with a neutral base, such as a tea from China or India, weak in personality but high in color for the liquor. Subtle or recognizable notes are then added to the mixture: a bit of Chinese Lapsang Souchong for a smoky touch, a hint of Indian Darjeeling for fruitiness, a pinch of green tea for freshness and lighter color.

A key factor is the time of day and the purpose for which the tea is meant. The classic breakfast teas are made up of Broken Assam, Ceylon and Indonesian teas in varying proportions, mixed with South India or Bangladesh varieties. Ideal for breakfast, these blends can be drunk with a drop of milk.* Afternoon blends are lighter, generally using only whole Ceylon or Assam leaves for the body, and Darjeeling leaves to add flavor.

There are also classic blends of China* teas, and mixes between China and India, green and black, mild and strong variations. Prestigious manufacturers feature house blends with tempting names. To find the tea that suits you best, let your sense of smell be your guide. CD

Blends being prepared by a tasting expert in Ceylon.

Boston Tea Party

The spectacular and symbolic impact of the Boston Tea Party, which took place in the port of Boston in December of 1773, went down in history as the first act in the war of independence that was to free the American colonies from England.

By the mid-eighteenth century, the settlers began to show signs of resentment to inflated English taxation. Patriotic rumblings could be heard in Boston, New York, and Philadelphia, where the majority of British merchandise arrived.

King George III's adoption of discriminatory tea customs fees in the Tea Act in December of 1773 was the last straw. Tea was the third most important import after textiles and manufactured products, and this was therefore a heavy burden. A boycott of English tea ensued.

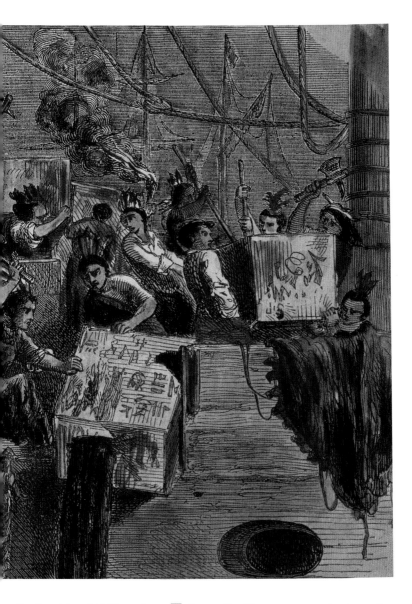

On the night of 16 December, three East India Company ships, the *Dartmouth*, the *Eleanor*, and the *Beaver*, after being held in Boston Harbor for several days, were attacked by American patriots disguised as Indians. Their cargo of tea was found floating in the harbor the next morning. Similar "tea parties" were subsequently thrown in Charleston, Philadelphia, New York, and Annapolis. SMD

■ Bruce Brothers

For over forty years, the East India Company was restricted to the Canton province of China* for its tea trade. Its world-wide monopoly thus left the Company at the mercy of Chinese producers. The Company therefore welcomed the opportunity announced by Major Robert Bruce's 1823 report of wild tea plants growing in Assam* in northeastern India.

American patriots attacking an English ship in Boston Harbor, December 1773. Colored engraving. Private collection.

The East India Company lost its tea monopoly in 1833, and American clippers* came to vie with its ships in the port of Canton. The Tea Committee, founded in 1834 by Lord Bentick to associate seven Company agents with eminent Indians, agreed to cultivate tea in the then-British colony of India. Chinese plants were acquired, but did not flourish in the new environment. Conveniently, the Tea Committee had concurrently dispatched Charles Alexander Bruce, to attempt growing the indigenous tea strain his brother had cited. In the space of four years, viable tea exploitation was established in what had been a hostile and humid jungle. In 1839, the *Calcutta* reached London with twelve cases of Assam tea on board. The Mincing Lane brokers considered this a great triumph—the British Empire was finally the proud producer of its own tea. SMD

■ Camellia sinensis

Camellia sinensis is the sole species of tea grown today. It consists of two main varieties, China* and Assam,* and a number of hybrids. In the wild the hardy Chinese plant stands six to nine feet high and lives for over a hundred years. Assam plants can reach up to sixty feet, but have a life span of under fifty years. To facilitate gathering, plants are pruned to between three and four and a half feet. They are grown from cuttings in nurseries with branch-covered roofs. The shrubs' evergreen leaves, tapered and dentate, are deep-colored and shiny on the top surface, lighter and matte

A Tea Branch in Flower, 1866. Engraving. Natural History Museum, London.

Root system of a Ceylon tea plant.

Women Gathered around a Samovar. Persia, nineteenth century. Victoria and Albert Museum, London.

in texture on the underside. The small white petals of the flower spread around a yellow pistil. The newly sprouted leaves and the buds are covered by a fine white down called *pakho* in Chinese. The term Pekoe comes from this word (see Classification). AS

Caravan

The silk route, which linked China to the Roman Empire beginning in the first century A.D. was also the green tea route. Tea was initially drunk only by caravan traders, who introduced it along the route at oases and encampments. Unlike the cargoes of silk, spice, and precious stones, tea was not in demand in Europe, and was the object of occasional exchange rather than commercial trading. Whether on the long Caucasian route to Byzantium or the Persian route to the Mediterranean, the caravans all traversed Central Asia. For centuries, Afghanistan was the hub of Chinese commerce with the Middle East. It was accordingly one of the first countries west of China to be won over by tea, which remains the national beverage to this day.

In his ninth-century *Relations of China and India*, the Arab merchant Sulyman describes a "bitter herb with more leaves and a stronger scent than clover. Boiling water is poured over it." Following the fourteenth-century expansion of the Ottoman Empire, caravan commerce was reestablished, and tea came into greater circulation. This gave rise to trading centers such as the town of Ispahan in modern-day Iran. It is on the authority of the Persian Hadji Mohammed that the Venetian Gianbattista Ramusio makes mention, in his *Navigatione e Viaggi*, of the existence of an herb used for infusions, which originated in China and was unknown in Europe. SMD

■ Ceremony

The Japanese tea ceremony *Cha no yu* (hot-water tea) was originally a Buddhist ritual. It became a social gesture in the sixteenth century. Today this refined pleasure is shared among friends, or to honor esteemed guests. The ceremony reflects the Japanese art of living, marked by aestheticism and Zen sensibility. According to the rules of the art, it takes place in a special pavilion, or *chashitsu*, which is reached via a winding garden path symbolic of a mountain path. Only natural materials are traditionally present in the tea house: wood, paper panels, tatami mats. The austere lines and the absence of furnishings evoke the simplicity of a hermit's retreat. The alcove (*tokonoma*) contains a painted scroll (*kakemono*), a few flowers placed in a vase (*chabana*), and a central sunken hearth for the kettle.

First, a light meal is served. Then the *Matcha* (powdered Gyokuro green* tea) is whipped with hot water to make the *koicha* tea. The instruments used are elegant in their materials and forms. They include the enamel tea bowl (*chawan*), the lacquered tea box (*chaire*), the whisk (*chasen*), and the teaspoon (*chasaku*). The host serves strong, then weak tea.

The economy of gestures and attention to the infinite details of a simple act raised to the height of perfection are designed to allow each guest to find an inner sense of calm in a shared moment of pleasurable contemplation. Rather than serving as performers and spectators, participants act together to create an instant of perfect harmony, in keeping with Zen philosophy. SMD

*"Make a delicious bowl of tea:
Lay out the wood charcoal to heat the water.
Arrange the flowers as they are in the fields.
In summer, evoke coolness; in winter, warmth.
Anticipate the time for everything.
Be prepared for rain.
Show the greatest attention to each of your guests."*

Sen Rikyu (1533–1591), *Seven Rules of Tea.*

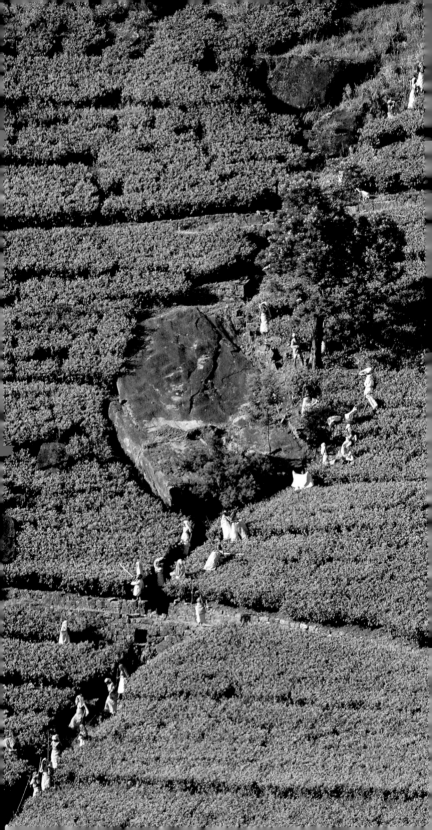

■ CEYLON

The teas of Ceylon (Sri Lanka) have every reason to please Western tastes. The British Empire's tea gardens* in this "tea island" were established to produce the black* teas they are known for today, with amber liquor and full-bodied, strong flavor designed for European palates. These teas are perfect with breakfasts and afternoon pastries, and go well with a touch of cold milk.* Such popular qualities make Ceylon the third producer of tea in the world.

The term "Ceylon tea" comprises six production regions—Dimbula, Galle, Kandy, Nuwara Eliya, Ratnapura, and Uva—and numerous gardens, each with its own flavor. Ceylon teas are generally selected according to their grade (see Classification) depending upon the desired strength, from a light infusion to a dark brew.

The Flowery Orange Pekoe teas, with their pretty hand-picked whole leaves and golden buds, are the most delicate Ceylon teas. Their mild, aromatic infusion is perfect for afternoon consumption. Among others, the Berubeula and Sam Bohdi gardens cultivate exceptional F.O.P.

Fruitier in taste than the F.O.P., Orange Pekoe is also an afternoon tea. Its leaves are longer and tapered. Kenilworth, Neluwa, Pettiagalla, and Saint James are among the top producers.

The well-balanced Flowery Pekoe, both full-bodied and aromatic, is suitable for both morning and afternoon. Fine F.P. is grown in the Dyraaba and Uva Highlands estates.

The Broken Orange Pekoe, with broken leaves, and Broken Orange Pekoe Fannings, whose leaves are ground, are dark and highly full-bodied teas for morning or after meals. A drop of cold milk, tolerated in all Ceylon teas, is recommended here. The Uva Highlands and Saint James estates are outstanding producers of both B.O.P. and B.O.P.F. CD

Nuwara Eliya, O.P.

Pettiagalla, O.P.1

Berubeula, F.O.P.

Nuwara Eliya Estate.

■ CHINA

The appellation "Chinese tea" is indiscriminately used by certain manufacturers and tearooms,* to designate a smoked Fujian tea. This creates confusion since the variety represents an insignificant portion of China's immense output, second in the world. There are more tea gardens* in China than there are vineyards in France and the variety of teas, from white* to red and semi-fermented* to black,* is infinite. While a number of these teas are reserved for local consumption, and never exported, what is available outside China is broad enough to represent outstanding variety and richness. Rare exceptions aside, China teas should not be taken with sugar* or milk.*

White teas, such as Yin Zhen (Silver Needles) and Pai Mu Tan, require an experienced palate. They are rare and often expensive.

Green China teas are among the world's finest. The delicately flavored Shi Feng (Lion's Peak), Dong Yang Dong Bai, with its subtle floral taste, and the renowned Pi Lo Chun (Spiral of Spring Jade) are precious and rare, available only from the finest dealers. More affordable are Lung Ching (Dragon's Well), reputed to stave off tiredness, Gu Zhang Mao Jian, with its scent of wet earth, Xia Zhou Bi Feng, with its vegetal flavor, and Ping Cha. These daytime teas are smooth and refreshing.

Semi-fermented Oolong teas are not heavily exported, possibly because their woodsy flavor is the opposite of the tannic taste popularized in the West by the British. The most readily found is Ti Kuan Yin, a refined evening tea.

China black teas, lower in theine* than their India counterparts, are most common in the West. Among non-smoky black teas, Keemuns are distinguished by their orchid aroma and mild sweet flavor. Keemun is a perfect afternoon tea. Yunnan tea's rare combination of aroma and strength merit its nickname, "the mocha of tea." The only Chinese tea that can take a drop of milk, Yunnan, is ideal for breakfast. Lapsang Souchong is a well-known example of a smoky variety of tea, well-suited to both salty and spicy dishes. CD

Yunnan imperial, T.G.F.O.P.

Hyson

Kwai Flower

Yunnan tea estate.

■ CLASSIFICATION: DECODING THE FLAVOR OF BLACK TEA

Over the years, experts have developed a classification system for black* tea based on leaf grades and strength.

Among the most subtly favored whole-leaf black teas is Flowery Orange Pekoe (F.O.P.). The word Pekoe comes from the Chinese *Pakho*, for a newborn's hair, referring by association to the down-covered buds. The term Orange comes from the princes of Orange, a region of the Netherlands, and has no relation to the color or flavor. This allusion to the noble quality of the tea was probably introduced by Dutch merchants. F.O.P. leaves are gathered* carefully and early, consisting strictly of unopened buds and the first two leaves below. The leaves are finely rolled lengthwise and mixed with the golden bud tips. The quantity of tips determines the tea's quality and price. The level ranges upwards from Golden Flowery Orange Pekoe (G.F.O.P.) to Tippy Golden Flowery Orange Pekoe (T.G.F.O.P.) to Finest Tippy Golden Flowery Orange Pekoe (F.T.G.F.O.P.) to Special Finest Tippy Golden Flowery Orange Pekoe (S.F.T.G.F.O.P.). All Flowery Orange Pekoes make light aromatic teas perfect for afternoon drinking. The same is true of Orange Pekoe (O.P.), which results from an equally fine but later harvest, at a stage when the plant no longer bears such tender tips.

Breakfast tea drinkers should choose a broken-leaf black tea for its strong tannic flavor. The finest broken-leaf varieties are produced with superior leaves and may contain tips. They include Broken Orange Pekoe (B.O.P.), Flowery Broken Orange Pekoe (F.B.O.P.), Golden Broken Orange Pekoe (G.B.O.P.), and Tippy Golden Broken Orange Pekoe (T.G.B.O.P.).

Made of crushed leaves, Dust and Fannings are usually sold in tea bags. They yield strong, consistent flavor.

This classification system applies only to black teas intended for the Western palate, for example from India* or China.* The majority of China* teas are F.O.P., G.F.O.P., or T.G.F.O.P. Their grade is not indicated. CD

■ Climate

Tea plants favor temperate wet climates with a rainfall of approximately eighty inches per year, and an average of five daily hours of sunlight. They flourish where long, bright days are followed by rainy nights, amid the fresh winds and the loose, deep, acidic soil of high altitudes.

Nearly forty countries, on every continent except Europe, provide more or less optimal conditions for tea growing. Foremost is India,* where the finest varieties grow in the northeast, on the Darjeeling* mountains and in the wet Brahmaputra valley of Assam.* In China,* the world's second producer, tea is cultivated mainly in the mountainous, often fog-covered central and southern regions, including the Yunnan, Sichuan, Zhejiang, and Anhui provinces. On the island of Ceylon* (Sri Lanka), the third global producer, plantations occupy the high southern plateaus, terraced between 18,000 and 75,000 feet, and in the range of the monsoons. Tea is also cultivated in the elevated areas of Japan,* Formosa,* and Kenya.* AS

Above:
T.G.F.O.P. tea
Terai (India).

Left:
Tea plantation
between Kerala
and Tamilnago,
India.

Clipper.
Nineteenth
century,
English School.
Bonham's,
London.

Clipper

Do regatta enthusiasts realize that in visiting the famous *Cutty Sark,* in Greenwich, London, they are paying homage to the last vestiges of the famous tea clippers?

In the early nineteenth century, tea was transported from Canton to London in heavy pot-bellied ships designed to hold a maximum of merchandise. It took these "Indiamen" a minimum of one hundred and ten days to reach England via the African coastline. For as long as the East India Company held its monopoly on tea commerce, the delay posed no problem. With the Company's loss of exclusive rights in 1834, shippers began to favor speedier options, the sleek, swift-sailing clippers. The American clipper *The Oriental* breezed into the docks of London from Canton in only ninety-five days, proving the advantage of ships built for competition. Arriving first on the market, the ship owners gained thirty percent over their usual profits.

On 28 May 1889, eleven clippers set out in a race from the Chinese port of Fuzhou. Three months later, the two leading ships reached the London harbor only minutes apart, with the third place vessel trailing only a few hours behind, and the others coming in over several days. The opening of the Suez Canal in 1869, and the invention of steamers in the 1870s, gradually put an end to this heroic era. SMD

Composition

A newly picked tea leaf is eighty percent water. Just under half of the remaining twenty percent is non-soluble, and thus not absorbed in the tea. These elements include resin, chlorophyll, starch, and salts. The soluble portion is one quarter tannins, followed in importance by theine.* Tea is good for health, containing vitamins A, B, and above all the anti-oxidant vitamin E.

A cup of tea is rich in minerals, including up to 0.3 milligrams of cavity-fighting fluoride, and traces of iron, copper, potassium, calcium, magnesium, as well as aluminum, nickel, zinc, and sodium. AS

■ Conditioning

The finest tea is invariably sold in bulk, in metal containers or hermetically sealed packages. For a variety of reasons, only inferior tea is available in today's widely used paper tea bags. The single-serving bags are too small to contain whole leaves, necessitating crushing, which yields stronger, more bitter tea, which however, suits many people's taste.

To offset these drawbacks, quality manufacturers have begun to offer larger, hand-sewn muslin tea bags. The muslin does not affect the tea's taste, and hand fabrication avoids breaking the leaves, allowing fine varieties to be made conveniently available. AS

■ Conservation

Tea is a delicate natural commodity. Its subtle flavors are perishable and ephemeral, subject to the vagaries of air, damp, odors, light, and heat. The best way to store tea is in a hermetic, opaque, and odor-free container, such as classic metal tins or ceramic jars. A lightly flavored tea should not be stored in a container that has previously held a smoky or aromatic strain.

In warm climates, the air-tight container can be refrigerated, as is common in Japan. If properly handled, all tea, including the fragile semi-fermented* and green* varieties, have a shelf-life of several months. It is, however, a good idea to buy smaller quantities regularly from the principal manufacturers, as their stock is regularly replenished. AS

Henri Cartier-Bresson. *Peking Tea House*, 1948.

■ Consumption

Tea is popular worldwide, with some thousand billion cups drunk per year. With an annual per capita consumption of seven pounds a year, the Republic of Ireland (Eire) holds the record, followed by the United Kingdom (a little over five and three quarter pounds per person annually), Qatar (five pounds), and Turkey (four and three quarter pounds). China* is somewhere at the top of the list, but no statistics are available. Japan comes after these foremost consumers, followed by Arab countries formerly under British rule. AS

Reproduction of nineteenth-century tea containers. Mariage Frères, Paris.

■ DARJEELING:
The Queen of Indian Teas

Often considered the most precious black* tea, Darjeeling is grown in the environs of a town which bears the same name, in the Himalayas of northeast India. Its flavor is subtle and refined. Among the most renowned of the eighty-three Darjeeling gardens* are Ambootia, Castleton, Gielle, Jungpana, Margaret's Hope, Namring, Orange Valley, Puttabong, and Tukdah. Darjeeling's excellence comes from a mixture of climatic conditions, altitude, inherited British know-how, and an insistence on quality over quantity. Their wide variety makes for a whole universe of Darjeeling teas. This diversity is the result of the expert blending of Assam and China plants in accordance with several crucial factors, including the related play of wind and rain (see Climate) on a garden's altitude and exposure, and the subtle variables linked to the time of harvest. Spring or first flush tea is light, floral, and aromatic, the second flush summer yield is more full-bodied and fruity, and the autumn third flush is characteristically dark, with a deep, complex aroma. The more recent white, green, and semi-fermented Darjeeling teas are still minorities in this region dedicated to black tea. AS

■ Desiccation

Desiccation is the last step in making tea. This essential process halts the fermentation* of black* tea. The leaves are dried to a water content of under twelve percent to prevent molding, but with sufficient margin to avoid damage to the aromatic content by burning.

Desiccation takes place in a large machine combining the functions of dryer and conveyor belt. Temperature and time vary according to the leaves' water content. In

Ceylon, where this content is relatively low, drying takes roughly twenty minutes from 175–195°F (79–90°C). In Assam, higher water content requires increased temperature and additional time. Green teas are desiccated to stabilize the leaves' constituent elements, destroying the enzymes which lead to fermentation. In China,* small piles of leaves are left to dry in the air, with frequent kneading. Desiccation is almost always carried out by machine in Japan.* AS

"Tea's proper use is to amuse the idle, and relax the studious, and dilute the full meals of those who cannot use exercise, and will not use abstinence."

Samuel Johnson
(1709–1784)

Above:
Tingqua
(1840–1870).
Desiccation.
Watercolor.
Museum of Art,
Hong Kong.

Facing page:
Tea gatherer in
a Darjeeling
garden, India.

English Passion

According to legend, Queen Victoria inaugurated her reign in 1838 with a good cup of tea and *The Times*, two supposedly diabolical activities, which her governess, the duchess of Northumberland, strictly forbade. Perhaps this has something to do with the queen's subsequent support for the Tea Moralities, tea parties organized by charitable societies to offer a nice cup of hot tea, along with a rousing sermon on the evils of alcohol, to the homeless, unemployed, prostitutes, and paupers. In 1942 Winston Churchill stated that tea was more important to his soldiers than ammunition. The British say they could not have fought World War II without their steady supply of tea. German U-boats terrorized the Atlantic, sinking many merchant ships with their crucial cargo, but reduced imports from India* and Ceylon* still continued to reach British shores. Rationing was

"If you are cold, tea will warm you;
If you are too heated, it will cool you; If you are depressed,
it will cheer you; If you are excited, it will calm you."

Herbert John Gladstone, Prime Minister of Great Britain (1854–1930).

Ambulant tea vendor in Great Britain. 1937.

instituted. Stationed in Africa, along the route that brought tea to England via the Red Sea and the Mediterranean, Viscount Montgomery's troops more than once risked their lives for high tea.

At the end of the war, the new ultra-modern tea trolleys that appeared in English train stations were a symbol of economic and social improvement. SMD

Europe

Europe discovered tea at the dawn of the seventeenth century. The Dutch East India Company* (Vereeningde Oostindische Compagnie) was the first importer in 1606. Tea was consumed in Amsterdam, London, and Paris for its therapeutic qualities (see Health) as early as 1635. Towards the end of the seventeenth century, the English smuggled tea plants (Camellia sinensis*) out of China in Ward Boxes, designed by the botanist N. B. Ward. These portable mini-greenhouses were made of wood with a vaulted

glass top, and filled with the proper soil to preserve fauna collected from around the world by the British East India Company. Tea came to Germany via Holland around 1640. The German Royal Tea Company was founded in 1752, importing sixty different kinds of China* tea to the ports of Hamburg and Bremen. The Asian drink had taken hold in Europe.

For over two hundred years, Europeans drank only green tea from China and Japan.* The consumption of black* China tea beginning in the late eighteenth century remained minimal until the end of the nineteenth century, when India and Ceylon strains became available (see India and Ceylon). SMD

Nicolaes Muys. *The Ridiculous Gentleman.* Oil on panel. Boymans-Van Beuningen Museum, Rotterdam.

"Is there no Latin word for Tea? Upon my soul, if I had known that I would have let the vulgar stuff alone."

Hilaire Belloc (1870–1953), "On Tea," 1908.

Albert Anker.
*Tea and
Madeleines.* 1873.
Oil on canvas.
Private collection.

■ **European Literature**

Ubiquitous in the long traditions of Chinese and Japanese poetry, tea came to feature in European literature during the nineteenth century. However, tea has rarely been treated as a subject in its own right. Perhaps this is because it is so much a part of daily life that it is difficult to distinguish its influence. George Orwell is one of the few authors to have written on the subject, publishing an often overlooked essay on tea entitled "A Nice Cup of Tea." He remarks that sugar kills the taste of tea, and that the older one gets, the stronger one prefers tea to be. Perhaps the most famous depiction of tea in literature is in Lewis Carroll's children's masterpiece *Alice in Wonderland*, where the Mad Hatter and the Dormouse invite Alice to partake of an Unbirthday high tea. Spy story writer Len Deighton in his novel *SS-GB* imagined a world where England had been conquered by invaders who kept the population from rebellion by supplying them with rations of ersatz tea. More usual depictions of tea time are to be found in classic nineteenth-century novels all over Europe, including Tolstoy's *Anna Karenina*, Jane Austen's *Pride and Prejudice*, and Thackeray's *Vanity Fair*. Tea drinking also crossed the Atlantic, playing a key role in novels such as Henry James's *Portrait of a Lady*. MD

Exoticism

Although a few travelogues, including Marco Polo's well-known *Travels*, make mention of tea even before it was first exported from the Far East, tea did not catch on in Europe until the creation of the major maritime companies* in the early seventeenth century. The Dutch were the first to develop a taste for tea, followed by the Germans and the English. Company ships (see Clippers) imported silk, porcelain,* and lacquered wood objects as well as tea. The first grains of coffee from Arabia and cacao beans from the New World appeared during the same period. Along with their cargoes, the ships imported the word for tea in southern Chinese dialect: *tay*. Caravans trading with the East from northern China spread the Pekinese version, *cha*, to Persia, Turkey, and Russia.

Tea was part of the fashion for exotic products that overtook seventeenth-century Europe in the form of *chinoiseries* and *turqueries* which affected table and decorative arts as well as painting and literature. The success of tea has not waned since, with catalogs from fine tea purveyors steadily growing. Today China exports certain green* teas that were unknown in the West even a few years ago. AS

Fermentation

Semi-fermented* and black* teas are subject to fermentation, the fourth and most delicate stage of fabrication. Once the leaves are rolled* to release their essential oils, a mysterious chemical reaction takes place that determines the tea's color, aroma, and taste. No one knows exactly how these qualities are produced. Some of the cellular reactions in the process are still not understood or even identified. In fermentation, leaves are spread on broad slabs of cement, glass, or aluminum, and exposed to conditions of ninety percent humidity. The air must be kept at between seventy-two and eighty-two degrees Fahrenheit. A slight rise in temperature will give the tea a burned taste; a slight drop will stop fermentation. In this warm and humid environment, the leaves first heat up as the result of chemical interactions, then begin to cool down.

The tea technician must have a keen sense of timing. Fermentation should be ended exactly when the leaf stops heating, which can take from one to three hours. Too little fermentation makes for weak leaves; too much fermentation diminishes the aroma. Semi-fermented teas are put through the beginning stages of fermentation only, to create their special flavor halfway between green* and black* tea. AS

"There are few hours in life more agreeable than the hour dedicated to the ceremony known as afternoon tea."

Henry James, *Portrait of a Lady.*

■ FORMOSA

Tea cultivation is much more recent in Formosa (Taiwan) than in China. The first tea plants, from China's Fujian region, were planted in Formosa two hundred years ago, when the island was annexed to imperial China. Ideal conditions, including a temperature that never drops lower than 12°C (55°F), contribute to the flourishing plantations. Formosa teas are widely distributed and readily available.

The island is best known for its semifermented* Oolong teas. Lightly fermented in accordance with Chinese tradition, Chinese Oolong teas have a light, vegetal flavor. The Formosa Oolong teas, fermented to sixty percent in the Taiwanese fashion, are darker and fruitier.

Formosa teas are low in theine,* and ideal for evening consumption. They are best taken without milk* or sugar.*

Tung Ting is a Chinese-style Oolong renowned for its amber color and mild flavor. It can be drunk at any time of day. In the same category, Imperial Pouchong has a fine golden liquor and a delicate, subtle aroma.

Grand Oolong Fancy is among the best Formosa Oolongs. Its fine, fragrant spring-harvested leaves are mixed with white buds.

Formosa also produces distinctive green* and black* teas. The green teas include flat-leaf Lung Ching-type teas, twisted-leaf Pi Lo Chun-style varieties, and rolled-leaf Gunpowder* tea. The finest Formosa black teas are smoky. Tarry Souchongs are more smoky than their China Lapsang Souchong counterparts, and appreciated by smoky flavor lovers. They are perfect for brunch and hearty English breakfasts. CD

Grand Oolong Fancy

Tea junks in Toa-ko-ham.

Gunpowder Zhu Cha

Tarry Souchong

John Thompson. *Sedan Chair and Chinese Coolies,* c. 1868. Private collection.

Fortune, Robert

The English succeeded in growing *Camellia sinensis** on the island of Ceylon in 1839, but ten years later the tea produced remained inferior in quality. It took the English botanist Robert Fortune to solve the secrets of tea-making jealously guarded by the Chinese. Having spent 1843–45 researching rare plants in China, Fortune was enlisted by the Tea Committee to return on an undercover mission in 1848.

Fortune landed in Shanghai disguised as a Chinese merchant and accompanied by two Chinese co-conspirators. Traveling in a sedan drawn by coolies, Fortune set out first for the green* tea regions, where he observed tea farming and soils, scrupulously noting the leaf-gathering and processing techniques. During a stopover at a Buddhist temple in Kooshan, Fortune was served the best tea he had ever tasted, prepared with spring water. This is where he realized that the quality of the tea depends on the quality of the water. After returning to Shanghai, Fortune undertook the second leg of his voyage, through the black* tea regions. He visited tea producers disguised this time as a Mongolian mandarin, and was accompanied by a Chinese friend.

At the end of his journey, Fortune sent all the plants he had managed to gather to Calcutta, where he arrived with eighty-five Chinese specialists whose expertise proved indispensable to England. Fortune's writings on his time in China include *A Journey to the Tea Countries of China.* SMD

Fortune-Telling

Divination with tea leaves is a time-honored practice in the Far East. Tea-drinking has always accompanied meditation in China and Japan (see Zen). *Chaking,* the celebrated

William Paxton. *Tea Leaves.* 1909. Metropolitan Museum of Art, New York.

Tea Classic written by Lu Yu in the eighth century, makes reference to the religions of Taoism, Confucianism, and Buddhism. A meditative act in itself, the tea ceremony is followed by an analysis of the configuration of leaves left in the cup, considered to reflect the state of things at a precise instant. Interpretation involves a vocabulary of shapes with symbolic meanings, similar to the trigrams and hexagrams of the *I-Ching* or *Book of Changes*, the treatise on divination which was one of the Six Classics of Chinese wisdom. Anthony Wild's *The East India Company Book of Tea* (1994) cites an early twentieth-century account of the vogue for reading tea leaves in Western society. The author humorously predicts the fortune of tea bags: they would destroy this branch of the art of divination. SMD

France

Tea reached France at the same time as the other countries of Europe,* at the start of the seventeenth century. Its consumption was initially limited to a privileged few in Paris. Tea gained popularity with the arrival at court of Jules Mazarin in 1639. The future cardinal, who drank tea for his gout, introduced the drink to members of the French nobility. Tea slowly took hold over the seventeenth and eighteenth centuries with the fashion for exoticism.*

Like other novelties, such as chocolate and tobacco, tea was initially recommended for its curative properties (see Health) rather than for the pleasure of consumption. Scholarly treatises and medical theses from the 1640s were published to extol the benefits or denounce the evils of tea. The Marquise de Sévigné cites the princess of Tarante's report of the Landgrave of Hesse-Cassel who drank forty cups of tea every morning. "He was dying, and it brought him back to life before our eyes," the princess claimed.

Prior to the triumphal Chinese expedition of the French ship *Amphitrite* in 1700, the French were limited to expensive, low-quality tea imported from Holland.

Unlike in England, where it rapidly won the day, tea's popularity in France was hampered by its aristocratic beginnings and its price which long remained higher than that of coffee, still a far more popular drink than tea. Though on the rise, tea consumption* remains low in France to this day. AS

Louis Carré. *Tea in the Garden.* 1910. Musée d'Orsay, Paris.

Overleaf: Michel-Barthélemy Ollivier. *English Tea in Paris, at the Prince of Conti's Court.* 1764. Oil on panel. Musée National du Chateau de Versailles.

■ Garden

In the poetic vocabulary of tea, "garden" designates a plantation producing a tea that will not be mixed with any other, and that often bears its name. A tea garden is thus similar to a fine estate vineyard, with the equivalent of renowned vintages. To savor the tea of a garden is not simply to take a sip of Ceylon* but to relish the delicacy of a Pettiagalla, or the fruity bouquet of a Saint James from the Uva district. Connoisseurs do not simply

choose a green* China* tea, but marvel at the aroma of a Lung Ching or the roundness of a Pi Lo Chun. The universe of tea is infinitely rich and nuanced. Gardens are not necessarily small, and may extend to over two thousand acres. They are generally located at high altitudes, under ideal climatic conditions. Gathering* is never mechanical and is often done by skilled women. Unlike common commercial tea, garden tea is usually sold by weight, with whole leaves. AS

Tea gatherers in a garden of the Nuwara Eliya region of Sri Lanka.

■ Gathering

Throughout the world, fine tea is hand-picked. In Asia, this is rarely a man's job. The delicate gestures, dexterity, and patience of women are considered essential for high-quality yields. With two swift hands, women gather the top leaves from the plant's "gathering table," tossing them over their backs into a strapped-on basket.

Gathering varies according to leaf grade (see Classification). Imperial plucking, formerly reserved for the emperor of China's* tea, is still practiced in a handful of gardens* in China and Japan.* Here, gloved virgins gather only the topmost bud,

and sometimes the first leaf. In fine plucking of top-quality teas, the bud and first two leaves are gathered. More standard gathering comprises the bud and first three leaves. Plucking down to the forth or fifth leaves produces lesser-quality tea. In some countries, mediocre tea is grown on flat ground and machine-harvested. In Darjeeling, where the best India teas are cultivated, gathering goes by season: spring first flush in March and April; summer second flush in May and June; autumn third flush from September to November. Each gathering yields a different tea. The earlier in the year it is picked, the subtler the taste. AS

Right:
Tea gatherers in the Tamil Nadu region, southeast India.

"Thank God for tea! What would the world do without tea! How did it exist? I am glad I was not born before tea."

Sidney Smith (1711–1845)

Below:
Tea gathering in the Gifu region of Japan.

■ GREEN

Unfermented green tea is at the opposite end of the spectrum from black* tea, and not subject to its classification* criteria of body and strength. All green teas are distributed whole-leaf, whether flat (Japanese Sencha and Chinese Lung Ching), twisted (Pi Lo Chun), rolled lengthwise (Chun Mee), or in a ball (Gunpowder). The one exception is Japanese powdered Matcha. Formosa* and China green teas are processed differently from their Japanese counterparts.

High-quality China green teas are generally available in flat or twisted leaves. Their pleasing verdigris color is silvery in the case of great teas such

as Dong Yang Dong Bai, Shi Feng, and Pi Lo Chun. The infusion's crystalline color runs from pale green to pale yellow. Rolled teas, such as Chun Mee and Gunpowder,* are less prized. Mixed with mint,* Gunpowder constitutes the favorite drink of North Africa.

In Japan,* where only green tea is produced, leaves are greener and more vibrant in tone than in China, and infusion color is accordingly brighter, running from jade green to light yellow. The palate gradually becomes accustomed to these aromatic, fresh-tasting teas. Gyokuro, the most precious and expensive Japanese tea, is an acquired taste.

Matcha, the jade powder whisked with a bit of pure water into a thick, nourishing brew, requires initiation (see Ceremony). It is best to start off with a less sophisticated Sencha or the late-harvested Bancha varieties.

The quality of green tea is judged by its aroma, which should be complex, and the length of time the taste remains in the mouth. The occasional bitter note is highly prized. But if you prefer to avoid this nuance, quickly rinse the leaves before steeping. Green tea is taken without sugar* or milk,* at any time of the day, for its refreshing and digestive properties. Its high vitamin C content makes it unsuitable for late night consumption. CD

Boxes of Gunpowder tea in a Nilgiri plant, southern India.

■ Gunpowder

Gunpowder is a green* tea made of young leaves generally picked in the first harvest in April. Its name alludes to the fact that the leaves are rolled into little balls that "explode" into a refreshing green-yellow brew. It is used primarily to prepare mint* tea, because it does not alter the herb's flavor and color. Mint tea appeared in North Africa in the nineteenth century. AS

■ Health

The history of tea is closely linked to that of health. Legend* has it that tea was "invented" in China in the second or third millennium B.C. due to a chance event resulting from the hygienic custom of boiling water before drinking it. Tea was long appreciated for its medicinal properties, primarily stimulant in nature, due to what was later discovered to be theine.* It was apparently not until the Chinese golden age of the T'ang Dynasty (608–907) in the eighth century that tea came to be regarded as a nectar for aesthetes and gourmets. In Japan, tea was used from the start by Buddhist monks to sustain them through long hours of meditation, and had a reputation for prolonging life. It was also initially adopted in Europe for its stimulant, diuretic, and generally comfort-

ing effects, detailed in numerous treatises. In addition to theine, tea is composed of minerals, including cavity-preventing fluoride, and vitamins. In Japan, doctors recommend green* tea to pregnant women for its minerals, and to patients suffering from high blood pressure or prone to arteriosclerosis for a particular enzyme it contains. Another of tea's elements, catechine, is used in the treatment of stomach cancer. AS

■ Iced

In 1904, an English tea dealer named Richard Blechynden set up a stand at the Saint Louis World's Fair in order to acquaint Americans, familiar only with China* tea, with the black* tea of India.* In the sweltering summer heat, nobody was lining up to sample the scalding drink. Struck with inspiration, Blechynden put some ice cubes in a glass and poured his tea over them. Pleased with his invention, he served it to an eager public. Iced tea was born and went on to win over the United States and then the world.

A more recent development, freeze-dried instant tea, which is dissolved in cold water, is child's play to make but not a quality tea. The best way to prepare iced tea is to start with a whole-leaf infusion.

Tea can be brewed in cold water in the refrigerator for twelve hours, using double the regular quantity of leaves. The resulting drink will be weak and low in theine. Another method is to prepare the tea as usual, but with half as much hot water, then pour it over ice cubes. The original tea taste is better preserved in this way. Strong black* Ceylon* tea or scented* varieties like Imperial Russian* are often used in iced tea, but others, such as green* teas, are also refreshing. AS

Tea Revives You. Poster, Victoria and Albert Museum, London.

■ INDIA

Growing on the banks of the Brahmaputra, the slopes of the Himalayas, and into the south, Indian teas are known for their dazzling variety.

Assam* tea from northeastern India is, like its Ceylon* counterpart, dark and strong, with a round, spiced flavor. These are excellent for morning drinking, and a touch of milk* can be added. With a number of celebrated gardens, Assam also produces classic British blends.* Teas from the high southern plateaus of Nilgiri and Travancore are stronger than their northern relatives but have less character than Ceylon varieties. They are rarely exported.

Cultivated in the Himalayan foothills, its incomparably fine aroma makes Darjeeling the queen of Indian teas. Production at the eighty-three Darjeeling gardens depends on the gathering* season. First flush spring teas are light in color, with a Muscat flavor. This early harvest is eagerly awaited by connoisseurs. Second flush Darjeeling, picked from May to June, has more body and a ripe fruity taste. In-between summer Darjeelings are a combination of freshness and maturity. Third flush autumn Darjeeling teas yield a copper, full-bodied brew which can be taken in the morning, with a drop of cold milk, unlike all the other Darjeeling varieties, which are best drunk straight, in the afternoon. The top Darjeeling gardens are Castleton, Gielle, Makaibari, Namring, Orange Valley, Puttabong, Singtom, Springside and Tukdah. CD

Napuk, F.T.G.F.O.P. 1

A Tamil Nadu tea garden.

Darjeeling Namring, T.G.F.O.P.

Travancore Highgrown, F.B.O.P.

65

■ INDONESIA
Java's Black Treasure

The history of black tea in this archipelago began in the late seventeenth century, when Dutch settlers attempted to cultivate tea plants from China.* The initial failure met with success more than a century later when the Dutch government brought tea plants to the mountainous regions of western Java and eastern Sumatra. Plantations passed into the hands of colonists who skillfully developed superior quality tea with plants from Assam, but at great expense to Indonesian workers.* Indonesian independence in 1949 brought the departure of the colonists and the demise of the golden age of tea, as plantation owners never shared their secrets with the indigenous employees. For economic reasons, nearly all of the great Indonesian teas have given way to mediocre production for tea bags. The few remaining gardens, such as Taloon and Malabar, yield aromatic, smooth black tea. AS

Tea manufacture in Indonesia. Late nineteenth-century photograph. Tropenmuseum, Amsterdam.

■ Industry

The tea industry was born in the 1880s with the first machines designed to speed up and simplify rolling,* desiccation,* sifting,* and other manufacturing* processes. A concurrent development was the diffusion of tea in packets. Horniman was the first company to replace bulk distribution in this way, selling five million packets a year in the early twentieth century. One of the first major planters to adopt the new manufacturing and commercial techniques was Thomas Lipton,* the first tea industrialist.

Today, industrial tea dominates the market. It is available in a range of qualities, but it is by definition inferior to the tea sold by weight in the specialty houses featuring fine teas from the world's great gardens.* Cost and quality concerns make mass distribution of top quality teas an impossibility. Industrial-grade tea is a mixture of leaves from several plantations. It is manufactured according to updated methods which simplify and speed up production. The paper tea bag, the hallmark of this industry, is technically incompatible with good tea. AS

Tea gatherers in Java, Indonesia.

Following pages: Tamil woman separating tea leaves in Sri Lanka.

■ JAPAN

The world's seventh-largest producer of tea, Japan exclusively produces green tea renowned for its natural aromas and freshness. Tea is treated as a perishable foodstuff, placed in the refrigerator in Japanese households. The taste of green tea can come as a surprise to first-time drinkers. The pale greenish infusions are taken without milk* or sugar,* at meals or any time of the day. Due to the volume of local consumption, not all of the great variety of Japanese teas are exported.

The majority of Japanese teas are natural-leaf Sencha varieties. This pale green infusion, best in the afternoon, is available in a full gamut of mainly excellent teas.

The expensive Gyokuro (Precious Dew) is the most refined Sencha. It is shaded with mats three weeks before harvesting to promote higher chlorophyll content and lower tannin. This is the secret to its emerald color and exceptional mellowness. Cost dictates that it be saved for special occasions.

Matcha (Froth of Liquid Jade) is a powdered tea sometimes (Matcha Uni) made from Gyokuro leaves for use in the traditional tea ceremony.* Matcha is a concentrated, nourishing jade-colored beverage. In the West, it is used in sauces and sorbets for its strong aroma and vivid color. It is also a good choice for iced* tea.

Sencha Ariake is a top Sencha at an affordable price. It is produced on the island of Kyushu and has a subtle floral taste.

Two specialty imports from Japan are Hojicha, a roasted green tea with a distinctive taste well suited to Japanese meals, especially fish, and Genmaicha, quality green tea mixed with toasted rice and popped corn that makes for a pleasant snack. CD

Matcha Uji

Gyokuro

Hojicha

Tea garden in the Shizuoka region, west of Tokyo.

■ Kenya

Following its independence in 1963, Kenya, already renowned for its coffee, undertook tea production, initially to satisfy local demand as a result of English influence. With know-how acquired from British planters who had left the country in 1947, Kenya began to produce increasingly superior black* tea on its high plateaus. The uncompromising standards of the Kenya Tea Development Authority, founded in 1974, supported the creation of great gardens.* The most prestigious among them is Marinyn, which produces whole-leaf, broken, and golden-tip teas. With an annual yield of 210,000 tons and a per capita consumption of one and a third pounds (just over half a kilogram) a year, Kenya is today the world's forth-largest tea producer after India,* China* and Ceylon.* AS

■ Korea

Located between China* and Japan,* Korea cultivates a very smooth green tea.

Legend has it that an ambassador from the T'ang court brought a Chinese tea plant to the king of Korea in the ninth century. From this plant came the plantations that cover the southern Chirisan mountains. Tea soon played an important role in the Korean way of life. At the end of the Silla Era in the tenth century, an initiative tea ritual was developed for adolescents, practiced in specially designed, isolated mountain pavilions.

Praise of tea is a recurrent theme in the famous Tripitaka Koreana library of the Buddhist temple of Hae-In—tens of millions of engraved wood tablets dating from 1236. AS

■ Legend

The two most delightful tea legends come from Asia and relate to the origins of the world and of Buddhism.

At the beginning of time, Chinese emperors were also gods. One of them, Chen Nung, was particularly concerned with the happiness of the human race. He taught people how to farm, and created wheat, rice, millet, sorghum, and soy for their benefit. Despite these improvements,

Chen Nung still considered his work unfinished. The means for curing illness was lacking. So he invented medicine and recommended drinking only boiled water. One day, resting in the shade of a bush, the emperor boiled some water to quench his thirst. A gust of wind blew three leaves from the plant into his cup. Out of curiosity, Chen Nung tasted the brew of leaves, and found it delicious. He then named the bush. The Buddhist legend attributes the origin of tea to Bodhidharma. One day, after nine years of uninterrupted meditation, under a vow to live a life without sleep or any form of indulgence, Bodhidharma, overcome with fatigue, drowsed off and began to dream of sexual love. Upon awakening, the thought of his weakness plunged him in deep despair. He cut off his eyelids and buried them. They took root, growing into two bushes with the power of promoting wakefulness in every sense of the word. SMD

Harvest in the Meru region of Kenya.

▮ Lemon

A true connoisseur cannot conceive of adding even a sliver or a single drop of lemon to a cup of tea. This citrus fruit, fine on its own, destroys the natural color of tea and, unlike the orange, denatures its taste.

It is considered a sacrilege to add lemon to a subtle green tea, and illogical to use it in a good black tea, however strong, in an attempt to soften the flavor. It might be permissible to place a slice of lemon in an inferior-quality black tea, provided the resulting beverage is not called by the name of "tea." This practice is common in Western Europe.

Some maintain that the fresh taste of lemon complements certain iced* teas. Lemon is also an ingredient in some eccentric concoctions that contain tea, such as certain grogs. AS

▮ Lipton, Thomas

Thomas Lipton (1850–1931) was born in Glasgow, where his family had fled from the Irish Potato Famine of 1848. His childhood on the docks of the Scottish port may have instilled an interest in travel and ships. At the age of fifteen, like others, he set out to try his chances in America. Returning to Glasgow a few years later in 1871, he opened a grocery store with his savings of five hundred dollars. The key to Lipton's subsequent success was his ability to apply American marketing and advertising methods. He installed trick mirrors in his display window. The first showed passers-by their emaciated silhouette hungrily arriving at Lipton's. The second mirror, which inflated the viewer's reflection, showed the well-fed customer leaving Lipton's. Even for those who never set foot in his store, Lipton became a household name in Glasgow. In 1894, when he moved to London, Lipton was a full-fledged millionaire. He traveled to Ceylon, arriving just at the moment when the price of land was at a low following an epidemic of parasites, which had decimated Ceylon's coffee plantations, and he invested in land for tea cultivation. Lipton

Lipton visiting his Ceylon gardens, c. 1895. Lipton Archives.

Cases of Lipton tea being loaded in Ceylon, c. 1900. Lipton Archives.

launched a major advertising campaign for his new undertaking, coining the slogan: "Direct from the tea garden to the tea pot." Despite enemies and rivals, Lipton once again triumphed.

Lipton had a passion for sailing. He was a regular participant in the America's Cup, and launched several racing yachts, all named *Shamrock* after the first boat he carved as a child. Lipton never won the trophy, but the whole world followed the exploits of this eccentric millionaire. He died Sir Thomas Lipton in 1931, after being knighted in 1902. SMD

Loolecondera

The story of the Loolecondera estate is synonymous with the history of tea in Sri Lanka.* When it became a British colony in 1802, there was no trace of tea plants on the island—its economy was based on coffee. In 1839, Dr. Wallich, head of the botanical gardens of Calcutta, sent several Assam* tea plant seeds from India.* Conditions proved well-suited for tea cultivation in Ceylon, but did not progress beyond the experimental stage until thirty years later. In 1869, a parasitic fungus, *Hemileia vastarix*, decimated the island's coffee crops. Tea presented the best alternative for replanting. This was made possible through the efforts of James Taylor,* who set up a tea garden in the Loolecondera estate with outstanding determination. By the 1870s, Loolecondera tea was regularly shipped to London and Melbourne. Taylor's success inspired others to follow in his footsteps, and Ceylon soon became for tea what it had been for coffee. The Ceylon Tea Grower's Association was founded in Colombo in 1894. CD

Manufacture

After gathering,* the traditional fabrication of black* tea takes place in a five-step process. The leaves are first withered,* or spread out for softening. They are then rolled* for reasons of appearance, but also more importantly to liberate their essential oils for fermentation. Sifting* separates broken from whole leaves. Fermentation* is a process of humidification for one to three hours which determines the leaves' color and the tea's aroma and taste. The last step, desiccation,* stops fermentation. In the majority of today's plantations all of these stages, except fermentation, are done by machine.

Semi-fermented tea goes through the same stages as black tea, but fermentation is stopped after an hour or an hour and a

half. The strength and darkness of the te depends on the length of fermentation. Green* tea is not fermented. The leav are exposed to high heat to kill enzym which could start fermentation. They a then dried in copper pans over hea (Chinese style) or steamed in va (Japanese style). This is followed by desi cation, rolling, and sometimes sifting. White* tea is not processed or treate but simply dried and packaged aft gathering. AS

An East India Company Vessel Being Outfitted at a Thames Shipyard. c. 1660. National Maritime Museum, London.

■ Maritime Trading Companies

At the end of the seventeenth century, England, France* and Holland competed for commercial ascendancy at sea. The era of colonization was also one of navigation. Europe's newfound taste for exotic products considerably raised the political and financial stakes of maritime commerce.

While the sugar trade depended on power in the Atlantic, and spices on the Indian Ocean, the tea war was played out in a narrower battlefield. Up until the nineteenth century, Westerners looking to trade tea were restricted to Macao and Canton in China,* and Deshima in Japan.* The Dutch East India Company (Vereeningde Oostindische Compagnie), was founded in 1602 with headquarters in Amsterdam, the Compagnie Française des Indes Orientales, founded in 1664, was based in the French ports of Lorient and Nantes, and the British East India Company, begun in 1599, was based in London. The three were constantly wrangling for commercial dominance at various points in the Far East.

The Dutch were the first to import tea to Europe* in 1606, followed by the English in 1657 and the French in 1700. The English gained the upper hand, securing a virtual monopoly on exports from Canton. But China, suspicious of European expansionism, strictly regulated trade, requiring all transactions to pass through one of the twelve official associations for commerce with the "barbarians."

England found a secondary, illegal source of revenue in sales of opium from its colonies in India. Opium reversed the balance of payment in England's favor, weakening the ancient Chinese Empire in human and economic terms, as the new vice affected mainly the ruling class.

In 1834, the East India Company lost its monopoly on tea in China, but continued to make huge profits form the two thousand tons of opium it sold there each year. SMD

▪ Milk

The suspect custom of taking tea with milk is erroneously attributed to Madame de la Sablière in eighteenth-century France. With or without milk? That is the question...that should be asked only with certain dark, full-bodied, strong black* teas. For a true tea lover, the thought of adding even a drop of milk to green,* whole-leaf black, smoked,* or scented tea is a crime. Milk's only advantage is to soften strong, sometimes bitter brews at times of the day when a bit of smoothness is appreciated.

Should milk come before or after the tea? The British tradition of putting the milk in first is meant to prevent fine china from cracking on contact with the boiling infusion, but there are those who advocate adding milk first in order to obtain the desired tea color. The taste for milk can be taken to extremes. Alfred de Rothschild's butler used to ask guests what sort of milk they wanted: "Jersey, Hereford, or Shorthorn, sir?" AS

Women
drinking tea in
Marrakech.

■ Mint

Sweet mint tea, with its
legendary freshness, is the preferred nectar of North African
Muslims at all times of day.
This tradition is fairly recent in
origin, dating from the mid-
nineteenth century when
British tea merchants turned to
Morocco in a bid to offset the
loss of the East European

market. Green* tea was warmly
welcomed, as it softened the
harshness of the traditional
mint infusion without altering
its texture or flavor. Ever since,
fresh mint tea, amber in color,
is made throughout North
Africa with green tea, most
often Gunpowder.* It is generally prepared by the head
of the family. In traditional

Moroccan hospitality, two teapots are used and three successive, progressively stronger helpings are served. To increase its frothiness, the tea is poured from high above into small, often colorfully decorated glasses, presented to guests on a round, finely chiseled metal tray. If there is no mint to be found, absinthe or geranium petals may be substituted. In Tunisia, mint tea is often served with lightly grilled pine nuts. AS

Orient

In a recent book on tea, Han Suyin described the difference between tea in the East and West. In the eyes of this writer of Chinese origin, the English tea party, or tea time—with milk, sugar, pastries, and sandwiches—is a poor adaptation of Chinese tea drinking. In China,* offering tea is considered a truly hospitable gesture, and excellent for health. Tea keeps Chinese people constantly hydrated, lowers consumption of strong alcohol and overeating, and, according to the author, regulates all vital forces. In contrast with the West, where tea is marked by its aristocratic associations, in the East tea is a daily dietary staple for one and all, and a sign of hospitality even in the humblest surroundings. Chinese tea houses, India's* roadside tea stalls, Afghan chaikhanas, and the little cafés of Turkey and Egypt are democratic and lively—the opposite of tea rooms in Europe.*

Tea is served in half of the world's households, in the workplace, in trains, in nomad camps, and the most remote corners of the globe. Whether the simple green* or semi-fermented* tea of China, the powerful Assam* of northern India, the sweetened Ceylon Dust

Mandarin Pavilion and Garden, near Peking.
Colored engraving.
Nineteenth century.
Musée du Thé
Mariage Frères,
Paris.

drunk in Egypt, teas of the East are a source of a thousand and one customs forged by tradition. From the Mediterranean to the Pacific, teas are as varied as the people they unite. Only the Japanese, who raise tea preparation to a ceremony* with the rigorous rules of an art form, break with the everyday simplicity of tea in the East. AS

Pioneer

Following the 1823 discovery of wild tea plants in Assam,* India,* by Robert Bruce,* the English government sought to exploit this potential resource with a campaign promising prospective colonists an easy fortune. Many enlisted. The journey to Calcutta took six months, followed by a month in a steamer up the Brahmaputra River. The last leg of the trip was through the jungle, by elephant. Upon arriving, colonists were housed in unfurnished bamboo huts. After the arduous task of clearing the forest, the settlers selected their wild tea plants, and harvested them the following year. Seeds accumulated in

this way allowed for expansion and the planting of nurseries.

The pioneers lead a life of isolation. Their wives and children had been left behind in England, and the vast plantations were set up at distances from each other. Malaria, cholera, yellow fever, and wild animals were constant threats.

After several decades, the first colonists brought their families from England to join them, and a social life developed among them, making for a more hospitable climate. The bungalows gave way to palatial abodes. Hunting and country club society became established. The Assam Company built roads and ensured regular river transport. In 1881, a railway line was opened.

The planters' success was due in large part to the Indian workers. Their miserable living conditions and inhuman treatment led to comparisons between the Assam plantations and those of the southern slave states of America. This association with injustice meant Assam tea was long called "bitter" tea. SMD

Elephants clearing an Assam plantation. c. 1880. British Library, London.

Art Deco tea service. C. 1920. Porcelain.

Porcelain

Tea had been drunk in China for centuries before the first porcelain implements appeared during the T'ang Dynasty (618–907). Though the drink was alive and well before porcelain, it would never have attained the heights of refinement without this major improvement.

In contrast to the large, rustic wooden bowls "fit for thirsty oxen," small china cups promoted greater attention to tea and the process of drinking, as well as to the beverage's quality, which was perfectly preserved in porcelain. Whole-leaf tea replaced its inferior powdered counterpart in the teapot under the Song (960–1279) and Ming (1368–1644) Dynasties.

Porcelain and tea reached Europe at the same time, unloaded from the same ships in the early seventeenth century. Until the British discovered the secret of making porcelain a century later, fashionable tea was drunk in Ming-style

Far right: Chinese porcelain teapots. Early nineteenth century.

little blue cups without handles. European porcelain manufacturers, including Meissen in Germany and Sèvres in France, eventually took over. Initially sticking to Chinese models, they went on to create a variety of sometimes sumptuous services.* Its beauty as well as its preservation of tea's taste, aroma, color, and temperature make porcelain the perfect material for tea cups. AS

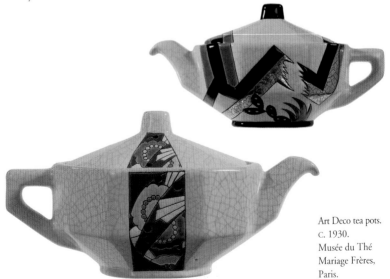

Art Deco tea pots. C. 1930. Musée du Thé Mariage Frères, Paris.

■ PREPARATION

A good brew depends on good water,* a good teapot,* and of course good tea. The rest is child's play. While the water is boiling in a kettle, the teapot should be heated. Since a good teapot preserves the trace of tea, a different pot should be used for each type of tea: black,* green,* or scented.* Once the pot is warmed, tea leaves are added. A rule of thumb is two and a half grams of black tea per cup: the equivalent of one rounded teaspoon for whole or broken leaves and slightly less for crushed leaves. Four to five grams of tea per cup are used for green tea. The leaves should be left for a few moments in the warm teapot, to release their full aroma. Barely simmering water should then be poured in. Water should never have reached the boiling point, since boiling destroys the quality of both the water and tea leaves.

A whole-leaf black tea should be steeped for about five minutes; broken-leaf tea three minutes, and crushed leaves two minutes. Green tea is steeped in Japan* for one to two minutes, in China* from three to five minutes. Semi-fermented teas steep for seven minutes, and white* tea, seven to ten minutes. The tea leaves should be removed after steeping. A built-in strainer is convenient. Otherwise an unbleached cotton filter is preferable to a metal tea ball which impedes the leaves from sufficiently swelling. Stir well and serve immediately. AS

Tea factory in the Nuwara Eliya region of Sri Lanka.

■ Production

With the exception of blending* and the flavoring of scented* teas, which are generally done by importers, all stages of tea fabrication are carried out in a manufacturing plant not far from the place of gathering.* The leaves must be rapidly processed in order for their properties to be retained. The plant may belong to a plantation, or serve several smaller growers. They range from old-fashioned factories in India* and Ceylon* to technologically advanced centers in Japan.* While tea gathering is usually women's work, processing is most often done by men, with workers and technicians putting in hard labor, often in dimly lit, sweltering rooms filled with the din of machinery. There is always one calm, well-lit sanctuary: the tasting room. It is here that the quality of tea from each plot and garden, and every grade,* is systematically verified. AS

■ Ritual

In China, the national drink retains its symbolic value. The time-honored custom of offering a bowl of tea to guests dates back to Lao Tse, whose disciples offered him the drink for comfort some time before 500 B.C. Traditional tea houses, comparable to popular cafés in the West, were closed

during the Chinese Cultural Revolution, but are now making a modest comeback.

Tea is linked to Buddhism in the Far East, and celebrated in Japan* with a Zen* ceremony.* In Tibet,* tea is the object of religious offerings and generous public distribution for holidays. The Russians' love of tea is embodied in the samovar.* This household item, a true sign of community, is also found in Iran and Afghanistan. In India, North Africa, and Arabia, tea is linked to hospitable traditions but not to specific rites. A symbol of relaxation, tea is drunk at home, at work, and in public places.

In Europe, tea is sometimes accompanied by all sorts of accoutrements, reminders of the nineteenth century, when both tea and porcelain were exotic, aristocratic tastes. Long reserved in China for nobles of the Middle Empire, like silk, china dishware is still a worldwide symbol of refinement. Its physical qualities are perfectly suited to the delicacy of tea, expressing an Eastern sense of the relation between container and contained. Nineteenth-century English tea time* and tea rooms*, which have spread throughout Europe, are to be found all over North America as well. Nowadays, tea lovers can buy specialist guidebooks to tea rooms in major cities, so they need never be without their favorite drink. SMD

Bedouin preparing tea in the Sahara.

"I don't care about immortality, just the taste of tea."

Lu T'ung, Chinese poet. Eighth century.

■ Rolling

Rolling, the second stage in traditional tea manufacture* after withering,* serves two purposes. The leaves are given their final curved appearance. At the same time, their cell walls are broken to release essential oils, provoking the complex chemical reaction of fermentation, indispensable for black* tea. Rolling

Above:
Phillips Ellis.
Tea leaves being
rolled by hand
in Darjeeling.
Late nineteenth-
century
photograph.
University of
Cambridge.

Preceding pages:
Packing of tea
chests. C. 1890,
Ceylon.

was once painstakingly done in the palm of the hand. This delicate, time-intensive process was simplified thanks to James Taylor,* the first tea planter in Ceylon,* who perfected a mechanical roller in 1872. Today, rolling is carried out in half an hour, by massive rolling machines composed of two metal disks that rotate horizontally in opposing directions. A portion of the leaves are broken in the process. They are then separated by sifting* and used for different grade teas (see Classification): Broken, Fanning, and Dust. AS

■ Russian

Long ago, only China* tea was drunk in Russia. Certain blends of black China* tea (Keemun, Chingwoo, Sichuan, Lapsang Souchong), called "Russian flavor" teas in France, were fashionable in nineteenth-century Europe. Today's most renowned Russian flavor blend was devised about fifty years ago by a French tasting expert. Based on the ever-popular bergamot-flavored Earl Grey, this tea adds the additional citrus notes of mandarin and orange in a blend of different teas. It is close to Earl Grey, with a little change from the routine.

Imperial Russian was an overnight success, soon available in a range of variations with different strengths of tea and citrus flavoring, and sometimes added spices. Today it is a staple of all fine tea catalogues, its name evoking the grandeur of the Czars.

Heady yet fresh, lingering on the palate, this tea is ideal for the afternoon or evening. AS

■ Samovar

In Russia, its former colonies and former members of the Soviet Union, tea time is synonymous with the samovar. It was invented in the mid-eighteenth century but came into widespread use a century later, with the spreading popularity of tea drinking. A samovar is a large recipient with a charcoal heater at its base, topped by a cylindrical chimney that passes through the water-filled container. The hot air in the chimney heats the water and maintains its temperature.

The *chainik*, or teapot, is filled with a concentrated tea, and put on the heating element. Once the samovar's water "sounds," (after it "sings" but before it "growls"), it is poured out of the spigot to dilute the concentrate. Samovars are usually copper or bronze, and can be electric these days. They can also be made of porcelain, crystal, silver, or gold. All the great Russian writers have evoked the household intimacy created by the samovar. Russians favor black* or green* tea, without milk. They sometimes melt a spoonful of jam or a lump of sugar in their mouths while drinking. AS

Interior of a traditional nineteenth-century Russian house on the island of Kizhi.

■ SCENTED TEA
An Eastern Tradition

The 1970s craze for scented teas in France, Germany, and Switzerland gave rise to an explosion of diverse and sometimes incongruous flavors. In the resulting confusion, it is often forgotten that scented teas are a refined Far Eastern tradition, and include great classics for afternoon enjoyment. Sugar* may bring out the flavors, but milk is to be avoided.

Earl Grey is perhaps the best-known scented tea. It is named for the British Prime Minister, Baron Charles Grey (1764–1845). He discovered the recipe on a diplomatic mission to China, and passed it on to a London manufacturer. The tea's popularity spread worldwide. Scented with bergamot, a Canton orange (*citrus medica*) Earl Grey traditionally blends black* China* or Darjeeling* teas, though green* and semi-fermented* varieties are sometimes used nowadays. Imperial Russian* teas, generally a blend of black China teas, are not necessarily scented. But its scented version is similar to Earl Grey; both feature citrus flavor such as mandarin and orange, along with bergamot.

Jasmine tea also comes from China. It is not a blend. Fresh-cut flowers are added to green or Oolong tea, imparting their scent. Whether or not the flowers are subsequently removed does not affect taste, but their presence is visually pleasing. CD

■ Schools

Tea schools are unique to Japan.* Up until the seventeenth century the "Way of Tea" (*Cha-do*) was not subject to explicit rules, but rather passed from master to disciple, with allowance for interpretation.

When the Tonkugawa clan come to power, it established a privileged status for tea masters in the social hierarchy. Sen Sotan (1578–1658) was the first to formulate his teachings into the tea ceremony,* to be studied in specialized schools.

Sen Sotan's grandfather Sen Rikyu (1522–1591) was a great tea master and Zen* practitioner. Sotan is said to have divided his property into three parts for his sons at the time of his death. Each piece of land gave its name to a different tea school: *Urasenke* (the school in back) *Omotesenke* (in front) and *Mushanokoji* (near the Mushanokoji Temple). The three schools still exist and carry on the traditions of Sotan and Rikyu. Diplomas are awarded by the great master (Iemoto).

The current master of Urasenke, the most popular of the schools, is Soshitsu Sen. SMD

■ SEMI-FERMENTED: OOLONG CHARM

Semi-fermented tea, subject only to the early stages of fermentation, is halfway between the strength of black* and the freshness of green* tea.

It is easily identified by its large, whole, unrolled leaves, whose visual qualities are appreciated in China* as much as the brew's color and taste. The semi-fermented leaf comes in a variety of fanciful forms which are endlessly described and discussed by Chinese specialists. They may be curly "as the dewlap of a powerful bull," swirling "like fog rising from a ravine," or evocative of legendary dragons. The name Oolong designates the finest semi-fermented teas in the Far East, and literally means "Black Dragon." This generic term covers several varieties, divided into two groups. Chinese Oolong, fermented twelve to twenty percent, is rarely exported, but drunk everywhere in China. It has a woodsy flavor and pale color. Formosa Oolongs are mainly produced in Formosa.* These are fermented up to sixty percent, and yield a golden-colored drink with a more "Western" taste.

Tea being sifted in Formosa, c. 1900. Archives of the Musée du Thé Mariage Frères, Paris.

The most popular Oolong in China and Taiwan is Ti Kuan Yin, (Iron Goddess of Mercy), a woodsy, amber-hued classic. Superior Formosa Oolongs include Grand Oolong Fancy, with its pronounced aroma and white tips, and the delicate, lightly fermented Tung Ting and Grand Pouchong.

Semi-fermented tea is perfect for all times of day and can accompany meals, though it is too weak for breakfast. It is low in theine, and a fine bedtime beverage. Jasmine, rose, orange, or other flower petals may be added. CD

■ Sifting

Sifting is the stage in tea manufacture* following gathering.* This step comes after withering* and rolling. A number of leaves are broken in the rolling process. A first sifting separates whole from broken leaves; the second sifting sorts them by size. Black* tea can then be classified by grade (see Classification): F.O.B., B.O.P., Fannings, and so forth. Although sifting machines began to appear in well-equipped plantations by the 1880s, sifting is still done by hand in some places. AS

Soluble

Soluble or instant tea is popular, mainly in the United States,* for making iced* tea. While improvements are steadily made to its quality, it cannot compare with good traditional tea. It usually is made by dehydrating a concentrated brew of black* tea. This is done either by pulverizing the liquid in hot air, or by freeze-drying.

Soluble tea is produced in some tea-growing countries, primarily India* and Sri Lanka (see Ceylon). Here the use of freshly picked leaves makes for better results. The tea is made either with fermented but non-dried leaves, or with a dry extract made from a fermented liqueur of compressed green leaves.

The leaves' appearance is naturally of no consequence for soluble tea, and their quality is not an issue. This allows for efficient harvesting. AS

Statistics

Nearly forty different countries produce a total output of two and a half million tons of tea per year. Green* tea accounts for five percent of this quantity.

Whether green* or black,* half of the world's tea is provided by just three countries. India* heads the list with 750,000 tons a year, followed by China, with 600,000 tons, and Sri Lanka (Ceylon*), where 250,000 tons are produced.

Kenya, a newcomer to tea growing, is close behind. Its annual production of 200,000 tons comprises two thirds of all the tea in Africa. Next in line come Turkey (134,000 tons), Indonesia (130,000 tons), Japan (86,000 tons), Bangladesh (52,000 tons), Iran (45,000 tons), Argentina (42,000 tons), Vietnam* (36,000 tons), and Malawi (35,000 tons). China is the world's foremost producer of green tea (403,000 tons), followed by Japan (86,000 tons), Indonesia (32,000 tons), and Vietnam (25,000 tons). AS

SMOKED: Unique Lapsang Souchong

The Chinese discovered a very subtle method for using Souchong, large and thick aged tea leaves that yield an otherwise light brew. The leaves are aromatized by smoking. This is done by skilled artisans. The whole leaves are first fermented like black* tea and lightly roasted on heated iron trays. They are then spread on bamboo racks placed over a pine or fresh spruce fire for a variable time, according to the desired degree of smokiness. Nearly all smoked tea is produced either in the Fujian province of eastern China, or in Formosa* (Taiwan). The lightly smoked Lapsang Souchong originally comes from China, and the highly smoked Tarry Souchong is made in Taiwan. Both countries produce both types of Souchong for Western consumption. Lapsang Souchong leaves are long and rolled lengthwise. In the West, they are on rare occasion broken, for example for use in tea bags. In this case, the brew is stronger and loses its special light quality. A classic variety is the China White Tips, a lightly smoked blend with added white tips. AS/CD

Russia

Georgia

Iran
Turkey   Bangladesh   China   Japan
                India   Vietnam   Formosa

Cameroon   Uganda   Malaysia   Papua
        Rwanda   Kenya   Ceylon   New Guinea
        Burundi   Tanzania
Equador Malawi   Mozambique   Indonesia
Brazil
        Zimbabwe   Mauritius
Argentina   Australia
        South Africa

Japan

Saitama
Shikoku
Kyūshū

Henan
China   Szechwan   Hubei   Anhui
                            Zhejiang
        Guizhou
        Guangxi   Fujian
angra‾   Yunnan   Formosa
djah   Sikkim   Terai   Guangdong   (Taiwan)
Darjeeling   Assam
        Dooars
        Tripura

India   Bangladesh

Nīlgiri   Vietnam

Ceylon
(Sri Lanka)   Malacca
                Malaysia

Sumatra

Indonesia
Java

Sites of tea cultivation

■ Sugar

Like milk,* sugar in tea is a delicate issue. Purists agree with George Orwell, the author of *1984*, who said that adding sugar to tea is like adding pepper to salt. Orwell compared the natural bitterness of tea to that of beer. If it is sugared, he pointed out, one tastes the sugar and not the drink. A comparable sweet beverage could be made by simply melting sugar in hot water, Orwell reasoned.

If one feels compelled to deviate from this common-sense view, it is best to stick to neutral white rock sugar which will not utterly disgrace the drinker nor the flavor of a strong, average-quality black* tea. It might also be tolerated in a scented* tea such as papaya or raspberry, which is already a sort of dessert in itself.

On the other hand, the same touch of sweetening would be an affront to a delicately flavored green* tea—unless it is flavored with mint and served, Moroccan-style, in a glass. AS

"The best quality tea must have creases like the leather boots of Tartar horsemen, curl like the dewlap of a mighty bullock, unfold like a mist rising out of a ravine, gleam like a lake touched by a zephyr, and be wet and soft like fine earth newly swept by rain."

Lu Yu (d. 804), Chinese sage, hermit.

■ Tasting Expert

Good teas are sampled by tasting experts, also known as tea-tasters, a minimum of five times. First in the plantation production* plant before packing, then by the tea broker, who sends samples to importers around the world. The importing expert tastes the tea three times: upon receiving the sample to choose and price the tea; upon purchase at auction

before shipping; and lastly upon delivery to verify that the product was not damaged in the shipping process.

Tea-tasting is a time-honored ritual. Dozens of little white porcelain cups, filled with brewing tea are covered, and lined up on a long table. Each is placed between an empty white china bowl and a small container filled with dry leaves of the same sample. The tea in the cups is poured into the bowls through the cover which acts as a strainer. Once the liquid has been poured the taster can compare the leaves caught in the cover with the dry leaves and the tea itself. The taster evaluates the leaves' color, shape, and elasticity, their odor in the infusion, the tea's aroma and color, and once it has cooled slightly, the taste. Like wine tasters, tea experts never swallow the beverage. AS

Tasting experts in Formosa, c. 1900. Archives of the Musée du Thé Mariage Frères, Paris.

British Pioneer in India, late nineteenth century photograph.

Taylor, James

James Taylor belonged to the admirable and sad group of pioneers whose courage and commitment made a fortune for others, not themselves.

In 1851, the young Scotsman signed on for three years as assistant supervisor on a Ceylon* coffee plantation. For five years, he worked wonders. Harrison and Leake, Taylor's Mincing Lane employers in London, put him in charge of the Loolecondera* estate to experiment with tea growing. Around 1860, Taylor obtained tea seeds from Assam* in India,* and set up a processing plant in his own bungalow, where tea was patiently rolled by hand. This homespun industry brought great results on the local market. In 1872 Taylor invented a leaf-rolling machine. The following year, he was able to send some twenty-three pounds (about 10 kg) of tea to London. Soon surrounded by a large, well-trained staff, Taylor took advantage of the sudden drop in coffee production on the island. He was instrumental to the economic success of Ceylon's new crop. Attracted by potential profits, major London companies

Previous pages: Tea gatherers in a garden of the Nuwara Eliya region of Ceylon.

began to invest, crushing the smaller enterprises in their path. Taylor, who did not own his estate, was instructed to leave Loolecondera. He refused, and died on the grounds shortly thereafter, in 1872. SMD

Tea room

At the beginning of the twentieth century, well-bred women in France, for whom it was not

proper to frequent cafés, preferred to take tea at home. This changed with the invention of the *salon de thé*. One of the first and most famous Parisian tea rooms, now called Angelina, was founded in 1903 by Antoine Rumpelmeyer, a pastry-maker of Viennese origin. The concept of tea or coffee rooms that also served Viennese pastries, while new to France, had already caught on in northern Italy. The difference was a matter of gender: In France the clientele was almost entirely women. The opposite of the lively French café, French tea rooms, described by author Roland Jaccard as "tepid, draft-proof homes for old people," are still in existence. Their old-style luxury, hushed voices, and stuffiness are a reminder of a more elegant past. AS

The Marquise de Sévigné tea room in Paris, 1934.

■ Tea Set

The traditional Western tea set, or tea service, includes a teapot,* sugar bowl, milk* pitcher, possibly a cream pitcher, a pot for hot water, and cups and saucers, all made of matching porcelain.*

Utensils for the Japanese tea ceremony.

Albert Lynch. *Ladies Taking Tea.* Twentieth century. Muséo de Arte, Lima.

The tea set came into existence with the eighteenth-century development of china manufacturing in Europe.*

On a more modest scale, a tea set can designate the teapot, the sugar bowl, a milk pitcher, and possibly a ewer for the hot water, made of something other than porcelain (which is indispensable for the cups), such as silver. In the British tradition, porcelain tea sets have little plates for afternoon tea treats. Tea spoons, sugar tongs, and possibly a strainer are used for serving the tea; tea and a kettle are essential for preparation.*

Such tea sets are useless in countries with different tea traditions, for example in North Africa (see Mint Tea), where tea is drunk in glasses. Utensils for the Japanese tea ceremony* include, in addition to the kettle and teapot, a long teaspoon, two different bowls, and a little bamboo whisk. Throughout the world and over the centuries, master artisans of precious metals and other materials have designed exceptional tea sets. To some true connoisseurs, the creamers and sugar bowls of these fine artistic objects are superfluous! AS

■ Tea Time

The privileged few in England began to drink tea sporadically between 1610 and 1615. Its popularity rose in the 1650s, with the opening of the first cafés in Oxford and London. These early coffee houses were

more or less reputable. One of them, Garraway's, held the first public sale of tea in 1657. At the top end of the social spectrum, tea concurrently made its court debut with the marriage of Charles II to Catherine of Braganza. The Portuguese Infanta shared her love of tea with the English nobles. Tea's cross-class popularity was rivaled by coffee, which appeared at the same time. Tea triumphed over coffee in the eighteenth century with the creation of specialized tea merchants—the first one founded by Thomas Twining*—the vogue of London "tea gardens" where strollers took tea, a sharp cut in tea tax, and the progressive disappearance of the coffee houses.

The Duchess of Bedford invented afternoon tea in 1840. This custom exemplified and codified the new British craze. Initially reserved for the elite, this gourmet ceremony consisting of tea, sandwiches, cakes, and jams, all presented on a precious porcelain* tea set,* was practiced in a more modest form among the other classes. Today subject to the constraints of modern life, five o'clock tea is still alive and well, though it may take an abbreviated form such as the office tea break. But wakeup time is also tea time—breakfast in bed is almost inconceivable without black* tea—and don't forget the afternoon meal called high tea. Drinking five to six cups of tea a day (see What to Drink When), the British are great consumers of tea, second only to the Irish. AS

Edward George Handel Lucas (1861–1936). *Tea Time.* Roy Miles, London.

■ TEAPOTS FOR EVERYONE'S CUP OF TEA

In terracotta or porcelain, for one cup or thirty-six, vertical or pot-bellied, long or high-handled, the lid hinged or separate: there is a teapot to suit every taste, custom, and budget—or several teapots. Because the teapot retains flavor, a different one should ideally be used for each type of tea: scented,* smoked* black, regular black,* semi-fermented,* and green.*

A good teapot, like a fine pipe, is seasoned with use. The interior is progressively coated with a brown layer. For this purpose, only terracotta and Japanese cast iron models will really do. Simple terracotta teapots are often among the least expensive, although the renowned clay teapots of Yixing, south of Shanghai in China, are costly and often the work of renowned artisans.

John Singleton
Copley. *Portrait
of Paul Revere.*
c. 1780.
Oil on canvas.
Museum of Fine
Arts, Boston.

To preserve a teapot's seasoning, it should never be washed with detergent, but rinsed with plain water and left upside down to dry.

The luxury of silver, the refinement of porcelain, the transparence of glass, or the simplicity of ceramic is a question of aesthetic preference. AS

■ TEXTURED AND CRAFTED TEAS
A Taste of Transformation

The veneration of natural beauty is omnipresent in Far Eastern culture. The symbolic link seen between art's power of metamorphosis and natural phenomena is expressed by the refined tradition of textured and crafted teas which began in the Chinese province of Anhui. The leaves are interwoven to evoke the form of a flower in bloom, often the peony, "queen of flowers," or a lotus bud, the emblem of Buddha, or stars, the home of the celestial deities, or pearls, born from moonbeams in the belly of the sea.

During infusion, the usually green* leaves open one by one, like petals, or all of a sudden, like a ray of light. Precious and expensive, these teas are for the magic moments of a tea-lover's life. They are prepared directly in the cup, with very hot water: 185°F (85°C). After contact with the extreme heat, the tea takes three to five minutes to unfurl, beneath a *chung* (bowl with cover), or uncovered, its aroma wafting directly into the air. CB

■ Theine

Theine comprises between two and five percent of the soluble portion of a tea leaf. The same alkaloid is known as caffeine in coffee and cola. A cup of coffee contains an average of 130 mg, while a cup of tea, like a glass of Coca-Cola, has only 50 mg. Theine is a proven stimulant, with negative side-effects only in the case of an extremely large dose.

Over 250 mg of pure theine, studies have shown, can lead to increased heart rate, pulmonary difficulty, dehydration, and irritation of the digestive tract. Five cups of tea in a row rarely provoke any of these reactions, since the theine is in part neutralized by tea's tannins.

Tea that has been brewed for a long time should not be confused with more stimulating teas, since brewing activates the tannins which counteract the theine. For those opposed to stimulants of any sort, it can be noted that China* tea is generally lower in theine than its India* counterpart. AS

■ Tibet

Tibet is a land of unique tea traditions. Tea found its way to Tibet from China as early as the seventh century. It was transported by yak caravans that took months to cross the high mountain trails to Lhassa. The typical bricks of tea were prized for their longer shelf life and

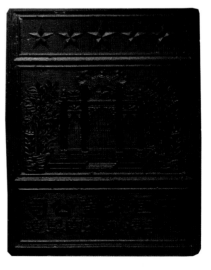

Yixing clay teapots. Reproduction of eighteenth-century designs, Mariage Frères, Paris.

Tea brick

ability to withstand the journey. In Tibet, green* brick tea is first powdered with a mortar and pestle and boiled in a recipient full of water. The tea is then poured into a wooden churn, and salt and butter (preferably yak butter) are added. The mixture is then stirred for a long time with a wooden mortar to obtain the desired consistency. This greasy, salty tea is often accompanied by *tsamba*, a ball of grilled buckwheat flour.

Another Tibetan tea custom is endangered by the Chinese occupation: the ceremonial offerings of tea made during major holiday celebrations held in lamaseries, which in the past attracted thousands of pilgrims. AS

Trading Post

In 1577, the Portuguese founded the Macao trading post, thereby dominating all trade, including tea, between China and Europe. The port of Canton, where all business with Chinese merchants was conducted, remained strictly off-limits to the Portuguese. They made no greater inroads in Japan,* where they were also the first Western traders. Their Jesuit priests' zeal for converts, and the profit margin the Portuguese sought to impose, led Japan to oust them in favor of the Dutch in 1638.

In Japan, the Dutch trading post was on the island of Deshima, an artificial land mass built in the port of Nagasaki in 1634 to accommodate foreigners, who were then forbidden to set foot on Japanese soil.

European maritime companies* were barely tolerated in Canton. In the mid-eighteenth century, the East India Company could boast of a dazzling fleet of more than a hundred vessels, and sumptuous headquarters in the heart of London. But in Canton, according to Lord George Macartney's 1792

William Daniel. *The Canton "Factories."* c. 1785. National Maritime Museum, London.

account, their factories "huddled one against the other...were rat-infested holes" where Europeans lived in a ghetto, denied all contact with the Chinese. SMD

Transplantation and Cultivation

Tea is a Chinese invention, whose discovery is the stuff of ancient legend.* Thanks to transplantation, however, tea is found everywhere, and gardens* are not limited to its country of origin. Korea acquired Chinese tea in the first century B.C., and it was in existence in Tibet by the seventh century. Bricks of tea were used in Japan by the eighth century, and and tea was transplanted there by the ninth century. Japan introduced powdered Matcha tea in the eleventh century, around the time that *Chan* (in Japanese *Zen**) Buddhism arrived from China. For nearly a thousand years, however, the secret of tea did not travel beyond these Far Eastern regions.

Russia began to import Chinese tea in the sixteenth century as a result of trade with Mongolia, but did not undertake transplantation until the nineteenth century, when the Russian Empire extended to austral zones favorable to tea production. In the eighteenth and nineteenth centuries, the English developed the consumption and transplantation of tea into a vast political and commercial empire. They discovered and cultivated wild tea plants in Assam,* India,* and also founded plantations in Ceylon.* Today, these two countries rival China in tea production.* The colonial influence of British culture in Africa and South America brought tea to these continents as well. Despite its proximity to India and Ceylon, it was the Dutch who first planted tea in Indonesia.* The earliest attempts at cultivation in Java and Sumatra date to the late seventeenth century, but it took a hundred years to succeed. SMD

Sacks of tea leaves being transported by wire to the processing plant in Ceylon. c. 1890.

107

Treatises

The earliest treatises on tea were written in ancient China*. The *Chaking* or *Tea Classic* is one of the earliest known and most famous. Written during the T'ang Dynasty by Lu Yu (8th–9th century), this exemplary work of Chinese philosophy mixes Taoist thought, Confucian ethics, and Buddhist metaphysics. According to Lu Yu, tea is an aid to meditation. In discovering tea, one gains insight into oneself and the world around.

Written by the Japanese monk Eisai (1141–1215), *Kissa Yokoji* or *Treatise on Tea and the Preservation of Health* also views tea as an aid to Zen* practice. Tea is praised for its therapeutic virtues as an elixir of life.

In the seventeenth century, tea was introduced in Europe as a medicine, and the first treatises on the subject were written from this perspective. In the eighteenth century, the Swedish botanist Linnaeus attempted to grow *Camellia sinensis* in Europe. This impossibility earned the tea plant a mention in the *Uppsala Amoenitates Academicae*, published in 1749. It was not until the nineteenth century that a discussion of the preparation of tea was included in writing on the topic in Europe, in J. G. Houssaye's *Instructions on the Preparation of Tea*. He furthered the discussion in his *Monograph on Tea*, which appeared in 1843. SMD

Twining, Thomas

In 1648, when Daniel Twining went to London to seek his fortune, he sent his young son Thomas to work for a tea merchant named Thomas d'Aeth. In 1708, the son started his own business in the Strand, a prosperous business district. Tom's Coffee House, as it was called, did so well that in 1717 he expanded with the Golden Lyon, where coffee and tea were sold retail.

London was brimming with such coffee houses at the time. There were at least fifty in close vicinity to Tom's, but Twining's was first to sell tea by the cup. It quickly became a meeting place for men of distinction. Women were not welcome in coffee houses, where beer and other alcoholic beverages were available. However, they could take refuge with a cup of tea or coffee at the Golden Lyon.

Throughout the eighteenth century, the Twining family business continued to prosper, evolving into a financial empire thanks to tea's phenomenal success in Europe.* As a crowning

Philippe-Sylvestre Dufour's *Traités nouveaux et curieux du café, du thé et du chocolat*, 1685.

achievement, Richard Twining (1778–1857) was appointed official supplier to Her Majesty Queen Victoria in 1837, and Twining's tea was again named by the Prince of Wales in 1863. The Twinings distinguished themselves as philanthropists. Thomas Twining (1806–1889), for instance, founded a museum dedicated to home hygiene, earning him the Legion of Honor at the 1878 World's Fair* in Paris. Twining's tea, essentially from Ceylon,* was sold by weight on demand. It was not until 1930 that closed packets were introduced. Twining's Tea remains a family business. SMD

The Twining's shop in Paris, c. 1900.

Henry Sargent.
The Tea Party.
c. 1820.
Oil on canvas.
Museum of Fine
Arts, Boston.

▨ United States

In the seventeenth century, tea was introduced to North America by the Dutch. Its consumption increased with the rise in European* immigration, and quickly become a staple in New England households. When England sought to take advantage of this by imposing heavy import taxes on tea, the colonists revolted (see Boston Tea Party). Once independence was won in the late eighteenth century, the new American fleet set out to do direct business with China* in the port of Canton. Tea imports rose dramatically, from six hundred tons in 1790 to six million in 1825.

Tea in early America was primarily green.* At the beginning of the eighteenth century, the Puritans favored bitter brews with butter and salt. The tea served at high society tea parties was flavored with saffron, iris root, or gardenia petals. This custom fell by the wayside in the nineteenth century, but tea-drinking did not. In 1904, the British tea dealer Richard Blechynden set up a stand at the Saint Louis World's Fair where crowds tasted iced tea for the first time anywhere. It was during this era that Thomas Sullivan, a New York tea merchant, invented tea bags: silk pouches containing a single serving. SMD

◼ VIETNAM

Popular during World War II, Vietnamese tea was grown mainly in the Tonkin highlands of the north, the central Annam range, and the high Mois plateaus. It became unavailable during the Vietnam War, and has recently made a tentative comeback. With food crops a national priority, tea plantations occupy a total of only around 130,000 acres. Annual production rose from 27,000 tons in 1983 to 36,000 in 1994. Vietnamese export teas are black* and slightly strong (for breakfast), light semi-fermented, and green.* There are also jasmine-flavored Chinese-style and Vietnamese-style lotus flower varieties. AS

Tea gatherer in the Da Lat region, South Vietnam.

◼ Water

For a good cup of tea, water quality is as important as the leaves. In *Chaking*, the celebrated *Tea Classic* written by Lu Yu in eighth-century China, the sage sets up a hierarchy of types of water, with mountain water at the top, followed by river and regular spring water. The Chinese masters were able to detect the different types of water in their tea.

Certain tea lovers today prefer particular mineral waters for their tea. The queen of England does not go anywhere without a supply of her favorite water for this purpose. The basic requirements are that the water be pure, fresh, tasteless, odorless, and free of calcium and sediments. Some tap water meets these specifications. If not, filtered or bottled water can be used. AS

"Indeed, Madame, your ladyship is very sparing of your tea; I protest the last I took was no more than water bewitched."

Jonathan Swift (1667–1745).

August Haerning. *Tea.* Mid-twentieth century. Private collection.

◼ **What to Drink When**

For some connoisseurs, breakfast, afternoon, and evening require different teas. For others, choice varies according to mood. Certain principles and false beliefs are worth mentioning. In his *Noveau Londres,* published in 1962, the French novelist Paul Morand noted the British habit of taking fermented tea before breakfast, and drinking progressively greener, less-fermented varieties as the day wears on. While certain black* teas, including Ceylon,* Assam,* Yunnan (see China) and late Darjeeling,* are perfect to awaken the taste buds in morning, vitamin C-rich green* teas may cause trouble sleeping, while their digestive properties make them excellent

◼ WHITE: A TASTE FOR CRYSTAL

A rare delicacy, white tea comes from the Fujian province of China.* Unlike all other teas, including black,* green,* and semi-fermented* varieties, white tea is unprocessed (see Manufacture). Once gathered, the leaves are simply dried. White Pai Mu Tan is affordable, Yin Zhen (Silver Needles), produced in a limited quantity, is one of the world's costliest teas. Its harvest, which lasts only two days of the year, can be cancelled if it is windy or should it rain. The imperial gathering is done by hand and consists only of new, down-covered leaf buds comparable in texture to edelweiss petals. The crystalline infusion is pale and highly refreshing.

Before investing in white tea, Western drinkers would do well to train their palates with semi-fermented and green tea. Price is no guarantee of satisfaction, and those accustomed to tannic flavor may be disappointed by the subtle white bouquet. CD

after lunch. Most teas are suited to different meals, according to whether the food is more or less spicy, salty, or seasoned. Afternoon is the ideal time to savor the subtler teas, such as spring Darjeeling, Keemun, and fine green teas. Stronger, scented* teas, for example Earl Grey and Imperial Russian,* are suited to snack time. Jasmine tea goes very well with delicately flavored cooking, and smoked* black tea is great for brunch. After five o'clock in the afternoon, a semi-fermented* tea provides aromatic richness with low theine* content. Expert tea blenders have developed special blends for various times of day: Breakfast Tea, Afternoon Tea, and so forth. AS

Tea withering in an Indonesian factory. Nineteenth-century photograph. Tropenmuseum, Amsterdam.

Ceylon Pavilion at the 1900 Paris World's Fair.

Withering

Withering is the first step in tea processing. After gathering, the leaves are softened in this way to avoid breaking in the next step, rolling.* Withering halves tea leaves' water content. The operation once consisted in simple exposure to sunlight, but quality and volume require closer control today. The newly harvested leaves are spread on stacked screens with about eight inches between each screen. A current of warm air is made to circulate between them for twenty-four hours. Climate permitting, the air comes in through open windows, but often, it is circulated by the use of fans, while both temperature and humidity are closely controlled. To save space and time the most up-to-date manufacture* sites use tunnels or vats, reducing withering to a six-hour process. AS

World's Fairs

Maritime* trading companies brought China* tea to Europe and its colonies beginning in the seventeenth century. Demand far outweighed supply, and prohibitive cost made this imported tea a luxury for the wealthy classes. The situation changed abruptly in the nineteenth century with the development of tea production in the British colonies. Robert Bruce's* discovery of wild tea plants in Assam,* India,* and the successful cultivation of Indian tea seeds at the Loolecondera* estate in Ceylon* led to larger-scale tea distribution. The late-nineteenth-century World's

Tea at a traditional celebration in Japan.

Fairs popularized tea consumption. The London World's Fairs of 1884 and 1886 introduced the new India tea to the English and international visitors. Ceylon tea was a hit at the 1893 Chicago World's Fair, where no fewer than a million packages were sold. At the Paris Exposition of 1900, the Ceylon Pavilion was thus described by one reporter: "The lovely colonial home with its bright awnings, the savory drink, the beauty of the natives, bronze statues come to life in their dazzling white loincloths, all that made this spot a huge success." Tea was on its way to popularity. SMD

Zen

Tea was the greatest ambassador of Buddhism in the Far East. Powdered Matcha green* tea was introduced in Japan in the twelfth century by Buddhist monks who had studied in the Chinese Chan (Zen in Japanese) monasteries. Tea sustained the monks through their long meditations and also served medicinal purposes.

Tea was far more popular than Zen in fourteenth-century Japan. It accompanied fine meals served in luxurious settings, and gave rise to tasting contests on which fortunes were bet. At the end of the fifteenth century the great Zen priest Murata Shuko (1422–1502) brought the spiritual value back to tea drinking; prepared with a few humble utensils, it was served in a minimalist setting. In the sixteenth century, Takeno Jo-o (1502–1555) developed this tendency into the tea ceremony, or wabi, in keeping with Zen precepts. His disciple Sen Rikyu wrote:

Though you wipe your hands
And brush off the dust and dirt
From the tea vessels
What's the use of all this fuss
If the heart is still impure?

Sen Rikyu organized the tea ceremony around four fundamental principles: harmony, respect, purity, and serenity. This practice is known today as the "Way of Tea." SMD

I N D E X

SELECTED BIBLIOGRAPHY

Blofeld, John. *The Chinese Art of Tea*. Boston: Shambhala Publishing, 1997.

Burgess, Anthony. *The Book of Tea*. Paris: Flammarion, 1992.

Goodwin, Jason. *A Time for Tea: Travels Through China and India in Search of Tea*. Somerset, NJ: Transaction Pub., 2000.

Pettigrew, Jane. *The Tea Companion*. New York: Hungry Minds Inc., 1997.

Podreka, Tomislav. *Serendipitea: A Guide to the Varieties, Origins and Rituals of Tea*. New York: William Morrow & Co., 1998.

Plutschow, Herbert. *Tea Master: A Biography of Soshitsu Sen XV*. New York: Weatherhill, 2001.

Tanaka, Sen'O. *The Tea Ceremony*. Tokyo: Kodansha International, 2000.

Willson, K. *Tea: Cultivation to Consumption*. New York: Chapman and Hall, 1992.

M A I N   V A R I E T I E S   O F   T H E   W O R L D

———————— Asia ————————

	DESCRIPTION	BEST FOR
CHINA		
• **White Tea**		
Yin Zhen	Premium buds resemble silver-tipped needles, crystalline infusion.	Special Occasions.
Pai Mu Tan	Pristine leaves (only withered and dried), clear infusion.	Evening.
• **Green Tea**		
Dong Yang Dong Bai	Flowery bouquet, full taste, very clear infusion.	Relaxation.
Lung Ching	Flat, golden green leaves, lasting aroma, delicate taste.	Afternoon or after meals.
Pi Lo Chun	Rare, jade-like green, mild.	Special Occasions.
Silver Dragon	White downy leaves.	Afternoon.
• **Semi-Fermented Tea**		
Fenghuang Dancong	Golden, smooth infusion.	Evening.
Kwai Flower	Large open leaves and Chinese laurel flower pollen.	Afternoon and evening.
• **Black Tea (not smoked)**		
Keemun	Orchid flavor, bright red infusion.	Evening.
Yunnan	Golden-tipped leaves, a unique spicy and rich taste.	Breakfast and with desserts. Milk OK..
Jiangxi Imperial	Rich, attractive leaves with golden tips, Deep red infusion.	Afternoon.
• **Smoked Black Tea**		
Lapsang Souchong	Moderately smoked over spruce.	Accompanying salty or spicy dishes.
FORMOSA (TAIWAN)		
• **Semi-Fermented Tea**		
Oolong Imperial	Lightly amber infusion with subtle honey and chestnut undertones.	Afternoon.
Grand Pouchong	Superior quality leaves, lightly fermented.	Daytime.
Ti Kuan Yin	Digestive with a complex flavor, amber infusion.	Evening.
Tung Ting	Orange infusion, light flowery flavor.	Daytime or evening.
• **Smoked Black Tea**		
Tarry Souchong	Very smoky taste.	Breakfast and brunch.
• **Green Tea**		
Gunpowder Zhu Cha	Leaves rolled into tiny balls that expand in water.	Afternoon. Traditionally mixed with mint.
INDIA		
• **Darjeeling**		
First Flush Darjeeling	Young tea with green-brown leaves, very clear golden infusion.	Afternoon.
Second Flush Darjeeling	Dark brown leaves, ripe fruity traces.	Afternoon.
In-Between Darjeeling	Balanced between fresh spring and ripe summer satisfactions.	Afternoon pick-me-up.
Autumnal Darjeeling	Large leaves, copper colored infusion.	Morning.
• **Assam**		
Assam First Flush	Very young, green-brown leaves, clear golden infusion.	Breakfast and afternoon.
Assam Second Flush	Attractive golden leaves, dark infusion, malted taste.	Morning or Afternoon.
• **Travancore**		
	Tea from southern India. Coppery infusion, full-bodied taste.	Morning. Milk OK.
• **Terai**		
	Tea from the plains south of Darjeeling. Deep-colored infusion, spicy flavors.	Morning. Milk OK.
• **Dooars**		
	Very colorful and full-bodied tea.	Daytime. Milk OK.

JAPAN • Green Tea	DESCRIPTION	BEST FOR
Genmaicha	Typical quality green leaves mixed with toasted rice and popped corn.	After meals.
Gyokuro	Pretty emerald green leaves, rich green infusion.	Special Occasions
Hojicha	Roasted green tea, brown infusion, very low in theine.	Accompanying meals.
Matcha Uji	Powdered Gyokuro tea.	Excellent in frozen desserts.
Sencha Honyama	Deep green tea, rich in vitamin C.	Afternoon.
CEYLON (SRI LANKA) • Flowery Orange Pekoe		
Berubeula	Attractive, golden-tipped leaves, golden infusion.	Daytime.
Allen Valley • Orange Pekoe	Highly aromatic infusion.	Five o'clock.
Nuwara Eliya	"Champagne" of Ceylon tea.	Afternoon.
Kenilworth	Harvested at the perfect moment, long attractive leaves, subtle aroma.	Afternoon.
Pettiagalla	Very large garden south of Dimbula, strong aroma, fruity taste.	Five o'clock.
• Flowery Pekoe		
Dyraaba	Full-bodied and full-flavored.	Morning.
Uva Highlands • Broken Orange Pekoe	Attractive rolled leaves from the high plateaus.	Morning.
Aislaby	Tea from the high plateaus. Coppery aromatic infusion.	Morning.
Uva Highlands • Broken Orange Pekoe Fannings	Very flavorful tea with a well-rounded taste.	Morning
Uva Highlands	Crushed high quality leaves, aromatic and strong.	Morning, delicious with milk.
Dyraaba	Crushed leaves from a famous garden. Full-bodied and flavorful.	Morning and after meals: replaces coffee.

Africa

CAMEROON		
Mont Cameroun, B.O.P.F.	High altitude black tea, malted taste, aromatic and strongly colored.	Morning. Milk OK.
KENYA		
Marinyn, G.F.O.P.	Kenya's finest black tea.	Daytime.
MALAWI		
Namingomba, B.O.P.	Black tea, full-bodied.	Breakfast.

Asia Minor

GEORGIA		
Georgian, O.P.	Fine leaves, dark color.	Evening.
Georgian, B.O.P.	Broken-leaved tea, slightly full body.	Morning. Milk OK.
IRAN		
Caucasus, O.P.	Red infusion, a light tea.	Afternoon, without sugar or milk.
TURKEY		
Rize, O.P.	From the Black Sea region. Fine leaves, sweet taste.	Evening.
Rize, B.O.P.	Tea from northern Turkey. Perfect for samovars.	Morning.

South America

ARGENTINA		
Misiones, B.O.P.	Black tea, broken leaves, very dark infusion.	Morning, with milk.
BRAZIL		
Sao Paulo, B.O.P.	Black tea. Strong infusion.	Breakfast.
ECUADOR		
Aproandes, B.O.P.	Black tea, broken leaves, very aromatic.	Waking you up.

Scented Classics

Earl Grey	Chinese or Indian Black tea with bergamot.	Afternoon. Can be sweetened.
Jasmine teas	Chinese Green Tea with jasmine flowers.	Afternoon or evening.

INFUSION CHART

China and Formosa	measure for one cup*	temperature**	infusion time
White Tea	¼ oz	158–185°F	15 min. (Yin Zhen)
			7 min. (Pai Mu Tan)
Green Tea	¼ oz	158–203° F	3 min.
Semi-Fermented Tea	⅛ oz	203°F	7 min.
Black Tea	⅛ oz	203°F	5 min.
Japan			
Green Tea	¼–½ oz	122–203°F	1–2 min.
India			
Spring Darjeeling	⅛ oz	203°F	3 min.
Other Black Tea			
Full Leaf	⅛ oz	203°F	5 min.
Broken Leaf	⅛ oz	203°F	3 min.
Crushed Leaf	⅛ oz	203°F	2 min.
Blended or Flavored Tea			
Black Tea Base	⅛ oz	203°F	5 min.
Semi-Fermented Tea Base	⅛ oz	203°F	7 min.
Green Tea Base	¼ oz	203°F	3 min.

* A teaspoon equals approximately ⅛ oz or 2.5 grams. ** Count approximately 7oz or 20 cl per tea cup.

Translated and adapted from the French by Stacy Doris and Chet Wiener
Copy-editing: Christine Schultz-Touge
Typesetting: Claude-Olivier Four
Color separation: Pollina S.A., France

Originally published in French as L'ABCdaire du Thé © 1996 Flammarion
English-language edition © 2001 Flammarion

09 10 11 7 6 5

ISBN: 978-2-0803-0468-1
Dépôt légal: 05/2001

Printed and bound by Tien Wah Press, Singapore